Courteous Rebel:

Jesus' Model of Leadership

Angie L. Mays

WORLD
CLASS
DECORUM

Courteous Rebel: Jesus' Model of Leadership
Published by: World Class Decorum

© 2003 Angie L. Mays
Original research, ©1996
International Standard Book Number: 0-9717821-1-3

Scripture quotations are from:
The Holy Bible, New International Version (NIV)

For permission contact:
Info@WorldClassDecorum.com

Ordering Information:

Fundraising, Business, and Promotional Sales: This title may be purchased in quantity at special discounts for fundraising, business, or promotional use. We have a special email referal program for organizational fundraising. Please contact: *QuantitySales@WorldClassDecorum.com*

Educational Sales: This title may be purchased in quantity at special discounts for college textbook/course adoption use. Please contact: *EdSales@WorldClassDecorum.com*

Individual Sales: This title may be purchased individually from our website: **www.WorldClassDecorum.com**

U.S. Trade Bookstores & Wholesalers: This title may be purchased in quantity at special discounts. Please contact: *QuantitySales@WorldClassDecorum.com*

Dear Readers,

This work is based on a literary critical content analysis of the synoptic Gospels: Matthew, Mark, & Luke. This was based on a serious qualitative study from a leadership perspective.

I invite you to challenge your preconceived thoughts about leadership & consider fresh ways that Jesus was able to capture the hearts and minds of his followers and bring them to a new threshold, which has forever changed the way we practice leadership.

Sincerely,

Angie Mays

FOR MY MENTORS:

DR. LEE HESS
DR. RONN JOHNSON
PASTOR GEORGE TRILLIZIO

AND ALSO FOR MY LIFETIME MENTORS,
MY PARENTS:
MR. & MRS. GLENN R. MAYS

I am deeply grateful for,
And give special thanks to:

Dr. Christine Cecil, a dear colleague and friend who has
encouraged me immensely in this project and has provided
the reflective, supplemental questions
at the end of each vignette.

&

Mike Feller, my faithful editor and friend who never ceases
to impress me with his talent.

&

My dearest friends and family, who have deeply encouraged
me to finish this colossal project and have greatly blessed me
by providing their unfailing support, wisdom, and joy.

&

Jesus of Nazareth, the one who has taught me the most
about the essence of leadership and provided me with an
even grander example of how to live life abundantly.
He has always been the unwavering pillar of strength,
guidance, and peace in my life.

Introduction of the Courteous Rebel

Jesus truly was a courteous rebel. He committed himself completely to challenging the status quo. Jesus' thoughts were not conventional thoughts, nor his actions conventional actions. He crossed many social boundaries in order to create a movement that was inclusive and full of hope. He did not use defiance or violence to advance his cause; rather, he used a respectful and gracious approach to influence others. Treating others "respectfully" also meant telling the truth, which at times required a poignant exhortation.

Jesus inspired people to live by a higher standard. This standard called upon people to love their enemies, pray for those that persecuted them, forgive others, and live out their faith. How was Jesus able to create a movement that has influenced millions of people for over two thousand years and has inspired people to live by these higher standards?

One cannot help but marvel at the tremendous trust and commitment that Jesus' followers displayed. What could be so compelling that they would give up the comforts of home, make colossal sacrifices, and take countless risks in order to follow this rebel who burst onto the scene two thousand years ago? To begin to answer this question, we must first consider how Jesus was able to earn the *trust* of his followers.

Everything in Jesus' life was congruent. His message was consistent with his actions, characteristics, and relationships. The unwavering commitment that he made to his followers was compatible with his purpose and helped pave the way for trust-filled relationships. He brought meaning and purpose into their lives by giving them a vision for the future and a reason to live by higher standards.

Jesus cultivated extraordinary relationships with his followers. He invested deeply in others and personally attended to people and dedicated himself to meeting their needs. He created a cultural

climate in which his followers could flourish, and encouraged an atmosphere of openness, accountability, and equity. He used symbols and celebration to help his followers find meaning in their lives.

Once he had enrolled his followers into the movement through these trust-filled relationships, he motivated them to remain committed by encouraging them and giving them hope for a more fulfilling life. He pointed his followers toward the future and introduced the concept of delayed gratification, where they would be rewarded for their work in heaven. Jesus was interdependent with his followers, and empowered this carefully chosen group by actually sharing power with them. He treated his band of disciples with great respect, as he had individually called each one of them to be an integral part of his team.

The essence of Jesus' leadership was his servant's attitude. This enveloped his personhood, relationships, visions, priorities, and the manner in which he motivated others. Everything that Jesus did was done for altruistic reasons. He loved people and invested in them completely. Jesus met their physical, spiritual, and emotional needs, and provided them with a compelling vision, purpose, and plan, as well as, the courage to carry them out. This rebel was a transformational leader who loved and servedhis followers; and in turn, he still has millions of committed followers 2,000 years later.

1

Leadership Characteristics

of Jesus

Possibility Thinker

Spirit of the Law

Developed Inner-Self

Balance & Discipline

Humility

Courage

Persistence

Plethora of Emotions

Love of Others

Compassion

Characteristics of Jesus

*A*fter analyzing Jesus' characteristics I divided them into ten major categories: possibility thinker, spirit of the law, developed inner-self, balance & discipline, humility, courage, persistence, plethora of emotions, love of others, and compassion. To begin our discussion of Jesus' characteristics it is helpful to conceptualize him *in toto* before examining his individual characteristics. The most succinct descriptor of Jesus is the "courteous rebel." This term was coined by Stephen Neill in his book, *A Genuinely Human Existence.*[1] This label is appropriate because Jesus firmly and eloquently practiced leadership. Even at birth, Jesus' character was known; Simeon proclaimed that Jesus would be both a peacemaker and a troublemaker.

Jesus lived by a higher standard and challenged others to do the same. Inspiring people to believe in something greater and higher than their own mundane pursuits, he provided them with hope for a better life. Jesus also challenged the status quo with grace and courage and never backed down from his adversaries. He was unshakably confident, yet completely humble. Jesus presented his ideas to others without manipulation or hyperbole and he told them candidly of the sacrifice that would be involved if they participated in leadership with him. Jesus did not glamorize their expectation of involvement; he asked for a great commitment to much hard work and sacrifice.

Certainly, who Jesus was as a person and the characteristics listed above that he possessed were important to the leadership process. Jesus lived his life in service to others, and he could not be divorced from the disciplined, authentic, and self-actualized person that he was. Starratt[2] calls for the *postmodern* leader to understand the importance of humility, hope, compassion, persistence, creativity, and laughter. What Starratt asks for in the postmodern leader affirms our analysis of the attributes of a leader who had already lived in the days of antiquity: his name was Jesus.

One of the most comprehensive analyses of Jesus' leadership traits was found in Russell's book, *Christ the Leader*[3], which describes Jesus as balanced, confident, courageous, gentle, generous, honest, humble, joyous, just, loyal, patient, persevering, trusting, understanding, unselfish, loving, meek, sympathetic, and compassionate. Youssef[4] in *The Leadership Style of Jesus* found seven significant qualities that aided in Jesus' success as a leader. These qualities included: the leader as shepherd, being courageous, gentle, custom-breaking, generous, truthful, and forgiving. The four traits that Olson[5] indicates are essential to the spirit of leadership are: congruence between speech and action, courage, commitment, and compassion. Jesus possessed each of these characteristics and gave people reason to trust and follow him.

Possibility Thinker

Jesus viewed the world through a wide-angle lens. He did not come up with trite, narrow analyses. Jesus was a contextual thinker who looked at the bigger picture before taking action. This is evidenced by the example of the woman who used expensive perfume to anoint Jesus in the home of Simon the Leper (Matthew 26:6-12). His disciples looked at this as a waste of money; however, Jesus knew that this act was necessary to prepare him for burial. Covey notes that "creative people are observant, often seeing and expressing parts usually unobserved by others and giving things a displaced accent. They have the ability to hold many ideas and compare them; their minds are vigorous...."[6] Jesus saw many things that others did not see.

It was perhaps his courage to think out-of-the-box that set Jesus apart from those adhering to conventional thinking.

> The breakthrough in creativity often carries with it an element of anxiety—because the individual is forced to seek a new foundation, the existence of which is not yet known. Individuals engaged in the creative process are well aware that they sometimes must sacrifice some peace of mind and sustain some anxiety to complete the incomplete Gestalt.[7]

Jesus' courage to be a possibility thinker enabled him to accomplish much. He lived and taught others that "everything is possible for him who believes" (Mark 9:23).

Jesus did not think in small terms; instead, he saw possibilities in everyday situations. He saw long-range implications in his interactions with people. His perspective was global, not atomistic. Never confining his thoughts within legalistic parameters, Jesus told the man with the demon-possessed son that "everything is possible for him who believes" (Mark 9:23b). Jesus told his disciples, "With man this is impossible, but with

God all things are possible" (Matthew 19:26). Additionally, Jesus criticized people for thinking in small terms. He blasted the Pharisees for their legalism and called them "whitewashed tombs" (Matthew 23:27), and reprimanded the disciples for their shortsightedness (Matthew 21:32).

Possibility Thinker

Why is belief essential to bring about positive changes?

What does "all things are possible" mean to you
in a practical, tangible way?

What allows people to aspire to an ideal?

Describe a time when you felt constrained by the current state
of affairs and changed things for the better.

Spirit of the Law

Relative to this type of creative possibility thinking was Jesus' view of the laws and mores of his time. Jesus was more concerned with the *spirit* of the Old Testament law than following a rigid, legalistic interpretation of it. Instead of sheepishly complying with the simplistic interpretations of the law, he challenged them. Jesus saw a grander picture and recognized that there are higher matters of the law that should be considered *(Matthew 23:23-24)*. He detected some problems with the status quo and was not afraid to challenge it.

Jesus himself said that he came not to abolish the Law but to fulfill it *(Matthew 5:17)*. What he challenged was not the law itself, but the twisted interpretation of it by the Pharisees and the teachers of the law. Central to Jesus' teaching was the theme that people's hearts should be right toward God and they should follow the spirit of the law, not a rigid, legalistic interpretation of it. When the teachers of the law and the Pharisees asked Jesus why his disciples did not follow the tradition of washing their hands before eating, Jesus asserted that,

> "Isaiah was right when he prophesied about you hypocrites; as it is written: 'These people honor me with their lips, but their hearts are far from me. They worship me in vain; their teachings are but rules taught by men.' You have let go of the commands of God and are holding on to the traditions of men." And he said to them: "You have a fine way of setting aside the commands of God in order to observe your own traditions!"
> *(Mark 7:6-9)*

On another occasion, some of the Pharisees challenged Jesus about his disciples picking and eating kernels from the grainfields. Jesus responded with the example of David and his companions eating the consecrated bread when they were hungry *(Luke 6:1-4)*.

And finally, he told them that "The Son of Man is Lord of the Sabbath," not of mere human rules and regulations (Luke 6:5).

Jesus emphasized the point that it is the person's heart that matters, not the rules. In Mark 7:20-23, he told them

> "What comes out of a man is what makes him 'unclean.' For from within, out of men's hearts, come evil thoughts, sexual immorality, theft, murder, adultery, greed, malice, deceit, lewdness, envy, slander, arrogance, and folly. All these evils come from inside and make a man 'unclean.'"

Again in Mark 10:5, Jesus explained, "It was because your hearts were hard that Moses wrote you this law." And in Luke 16:15, he told the Pharisees, "You are the ones who justify yourselves in the eyes of men, but God knows your hearts. What is highly valued among men is detestable in God's sight." It is a complex pursuit to understand the attitudes of the heart, yet Jesus considered the condition of a person's heart to be the paramount issue.

Jesus did not subscribe to a simplistic understanding of the law. Instead, he approached situations contextually, and this rather unorthodox methodology baffled many who were used to living under stringent interpretations of the law. Jesus attempted to reframe their dichotomous thinking by giving them a tangible, applicable example. He said to them, "If any of you has a sheep and it falls into a pit on the Sabbath, will you not take hold of it and lift it out? How much more valuable is a man than a sheep! Therefore it is lawful to do good on the Sabbath" (Matthew 12:11-12). This was a practical example that was intended to help the hearers have a better understanding of priorities. Jesus posited that there are more important matters of the law and in Matthew 23:23-24, He declared,

> "Woe to you, teachers of the law and Pharisees, you hypocrites! You give a tenth of your spices—mint, dill and cumin. But you have neglected the

more important matters of the law—justice, mercy, and faithfulness. You should have practiced the latter, without neglecting the former. You blind guides! You strain out a gnat but swallow a camel."

Jesus viewed the world contextually and challenged others to evaluate a situation, determine the higher moral law, and then attend to that first.

Spirit of the Law

What does the phrase "strain out a gnat and swallow a camel" mean to you? Does this ever happen where you work?

Do you think leaders are entitled to exercise special privileges?

Are you a more just or merciful leader? Why?

Can you have mercy and compassion on employees or citizens who have no remorse or respect for a law they have violated? Explain.

How can people who choose to obey have total freedom?

Developed Inner-Self

Jesus spent time developing himself. When he was twelve years old he sat in the temple courts among religious teachers who marveled at his understanding and his answers (Luke 2:42, 46-47). *So why did Jesus wait until he was almost thirty to begin his ministry?* Is it possible he could have been investing in his own development and waiting for the right timing? After being baptized by John the Baptist, Jesus went into the desert for forty days (Luke 4:1-2). During this time of testing and development, he disciplined himself physically through fasting, and spiritually by refusing to give in to the temptations presented to him by Satan.

Jesus knew who he was and taught others to examine their own lives. In Matthew 7:3-5, Jesus asks his followers,

> "Why do you look at the speck of sawdust in your brother's eye and pay no attention to the plank in your own eye? How can you say to your brother, 'Let me take the speck out of your eye,' when all the time there is a plank in your own eye? You hypocrite, first take the plank out of your own eye, and then you will see clearly to remove the speck from your brother's eye."

He also called the Pharisees and the teachers of the law hypocrites and told them that they "clean the outside of the cup and dish, but inside they are full of greed and self-indulgence. Blind Pharisee! First clean the inside of the cup and dish, and then the outside also will be clean" (Matthew 23:25-26). Again, Jesus was seen attending to the matters of the heart while also addressing self-development.

Many authors agree that it is critical for leaders to "Know thyself" (Hitt,[8] Covey,[9] Bennis[10]). Bennis[11] proposes that the process of becoming a leader and the process of becoming a fully integrated human being are similar. Bennis claims that leaders

...know who they are, what their strengths and weaknesses are, and how to fully deploy their strengths and compensate for their weaknesses. They also know what they want, why they want it, and how to communicate what they want to others, in order to gain their cooperation and support. Finally, they know how to achieve their goals.[12]

It is easy to see from this description that Jesus was a fully integrated human being. He knew who he was and why he was here, and this extraordinary self-knowledge and awareness of purpose fortified his strength as a leader. Bennis also posits that "The key to full self-expression is understanding one's self and the world, and the key to understanding is learning—from one's own life and experience."[13] Clearly, Jesus fully understood himself and his world, and obviously expressed himself and his message articulately.

Bennis adds to Socrates' "The unexamined life is not worth living" by insisting that "the unexamined life is impossible to live successfully."[14] Hitt[15] echoes this point and asserts that a leader who does not know one's self is handicapped. It is obvious that Jesus was not handicapped by a lack of self-knowledge. On the contrary, Jesus knew exactly who he was. The first step in understanding others is to first understand yourself.[16] Olson[17] stresses the development of the inner-self as the foundation for properly utilizing leadership strategies. Some of the tactics discussed by Olson include: maximizing the impact of a message, assuming authority, reframing symbols, not judging others, and capitalizing on tradition. Due to Jesus' extraordinary inner development, his tactics had a much more powerful impact on his disciples and listeners. It is clear that "Jesus had a superb grasp of timing, of drama, and of the human condition. He knew precisely what actions and words would make the greatest, most lasting impression on heart and soul."[18]

Developed Inner-Self

What is it like to work with or be in relationship with someone who lacks self-awareness?

What is the difference between self-knowledge and self-absorption?

How can a leader develop clarity of purpose?

When was the last time someone gave you feedback for your own self-improvement? How did you take it?

What are five strategies you might employ to develop a deeper knowledge of your personal strengths and weaknesses as a leader?

Balance and Discipline

Jesus was a very disciplined man who gave tremendously to his community while maintaining balance through periods of rejuvenating solitude. Jesus led a very demanding life. People flocked to him wherever he went. Yet even when in the midst of multitudes of people, Jesus managed to get away to find solitude, to pray, and eat. Jesus knew the importance of rejuvenation to help him serve others, and maintained balance in his life through prayer, self-development, spending time with his disciples, and giving to his community. Covey notes that organizational effectiveness "requires development in all four dimensions: [physical, spiritual, mental, and social/emotional] in a wise and balanced way."[19] There are many examples in the Scriptures where Jesus' discipline in praying and seeking solitude for rejuvenation is illustrated:

> • *Very early in the morning, while it was still dark, Jesus got up, left the house and went off to a solitary place, where he prayed.* (Mark 1:35)

> • *They all ate and were satisfied.... Immediately Jesus made his disciples get into the boat and go on ahead of him to Bethesda, while he dismissed the crowd. After leaving them, he went up on a mountainside to pray.* (Mark 6:42, 45-46)

> • *Jesus went out as usual to the Mount of Olives, and his disciples followed him. On reaching the place, he said to them, "Pray that you will not fall into temptation." He withdrew about a stone's throw beyond them, knelt down and prayed....* (Luke 22:39-41)

> • *That day when evening came, he said to his disciples, "Let us go over to the other side." Leaving the crowd behind, they took him along, just as he was, in the boat.* (Mark 4:35-36a)

As the Scriptures demonstrate, Jesus took time for solitude and restoration, but he also remained flexible in responding to the needs of his followers. In Mark 6:31-36, Jesus tried to retreat from the crowd so that his team could get a chance to eat and get some rest. As the team tried to leave by boat many people ran ahead of them. But Jesus had compassion for these people, and even though it was late in the day, he resumed his teaching and then provided food for five thousand of them (Mark 6:37-44). Jesus also knew when to send the crowd away, as in Mark 8:9-10. After he had fed about four thousand men, he sent them away, got into the boat with his disciples, and left for the region of Dalmanutha.

Self-discipline is a characteristic that was evident in Jesus' life. Jesus knew his purpose and used self-discipline in many areas of his life to prioritize the demands that were placed upon him by God and by men (Matthew 6:33). It is noted many times in the Scriptures that Jesus sought solitude to pray when he was very tired, in the evening, and sometimes before it was even daybreak (Matthew 14:23; Mark 1:35; Luke 22:39-41). Covey advocates coherence, which is the "harmony, unity, and integrity between your vision and mission, your roles and goals, your priorities and plans, and your desires and discipline."[20] Jesus certainly had the "harmony" which Covey describes that was congruent between his mission and his self-discipline.

Balance and Discipline

How do you know when it's time to act versus when it's time to reflect?

What percentage of your time is spent in reflection compared to action? Is that balance working for you?

What does the word discipline mean to you? What's the origin of the word "disciple"?

How can you create solitude despite the hectic and harried pace of life today? What will happen if you don't?

If you can't say "No," your "Yes" will never mean anything. Do you ever accept responsibilities and say "Yes" when you should say "No?" Why?

Humility

*U*ndeniably, Jesus was a confident leader. It is noted that when Jesus went to Capernaum to teach in the synagogue that "people were amazed at his teaching, because he taught them as one who had authority, not as the teachers of the law" *(Mark 1:22)*. Part of the brilliance of Jesus' leadership was that he was completely confident and completely humble concurrently. Jesus proclaimed, "Therefore, whoever humbles himself like this child is the greatest in the kingdom of heaven" *(Matthew 18:4)*. In Luke 18:14b, he said, "For everyone who exalts himself will be humbled, and he who humbles himself will be exalted." Jesus was a humble leader who did not need to be exalted. In fact, he often expressed his opposition to self-exaltation and self-aggrandizement.

Jesus spoke out against those who made a show of lengthy prayers in public places and who schemed against widows, claiming that they would be severely punished *(Luke 20:47)*. Regarding the Pharisees and the teachers of the law, Jesus observed that

> *"Everything they do is done for men to see: They make their phylacteries wide and the tassels on their garments long; they love the place of honor at banquets and the most important seats in the synagogues; they love to be greeted in the marketplaces and to have men call them 'Rabbi.'"*
> *(Matthew 23:5-7)*

Jesus points out the lack of humility in this type of behavior. A humble leader does not seek outward recognition; rather, a humble leader engages in his or her spiritual acts in private.

Humility requires truthfulness, and Jesus' perfect example of humility was sincere, not self-deprecating or belittling. On many occasions (Matthew 19:19; Mark 12:31, 33; Luke 10:27), Jesus taught the disciples as well as the Pharisees to "love your neighbor as yourself"—not "love thy neighbor, hate thyself."

A healthy self-perception can reveal true humility. An example of this occurred after Jesus' baptism: "While [Peter] was still speaking, a bright cloud enveloped them, and a voice from the cloud said, 'This is my Son, whom I love; with him I am well-pleased. Listen to him!'" (Matthew 17:5). This event terrified the disciples, causing them to fall face down on the ground. But Jesus received this beautiful affirmation from his Father, and knowing his true nature and identity. He also showed he was truly humble and cared for his disciples for he came over and touched them saying, "Get up. Don't be afraid" (Matthew 17:7).

Leadership literature on the topics of courage and confidence are readily available. Other than literature which specifically focuses on the leadership of Jesus, the concept of humility in leadership is rarely addressed. Once in a while, one may find humility mentioned as an attribute that a leader wishes to acquire. Starratt[21] challenges leaders in the postmodern world to be humble in their leadership. He posits that "Humility does not imply lowered aspirations. On the contrary, leaders are challenged to see the agenda as a moral agenda, calling forth the best that is in us to reverse the tragedies of this century."[22] Just as Starratt notes that humility does not imply a lowered standard, many still have difficulty comprehending how one can fully embody self-confidence and humility at the same time.

Jesus was a master at being both self-confident and humble—yet he did not seek to be exalted. Jesus was not impressed with people who made a show of their exaggerated religiosity (Luke 20:46-47). In direct contrast to the self-important and publicly pious religious leaders of the day, Jesus preached that it is those who humble themselves that will be exalted (Luke 18:14). As was true of himself, he was concerned with a person's internal condition.

Humility

Why is humility the absolute cornerstone of an effective leader?

Describe one humble person you know.

What does it mean to "die to self?"

What kind of a leader would you be if you died to self?

What would you have to give up in order to be humble?
What would you get in return?

What stands between you and genuine humility?

If you were humble, how would you and others know?
Why should you care?

Courage

*J*esus' complete humility allowed him to courageously take great risks because he was not protecting a fragile ego. Jesus faced great adversity throughout his ministry and was tremendously courageous in his response to each challenge. Imagine approaching a demon-possessed man who was chained hand and foot and kept under guard. Jesus did so knowing that the demons could take over the man and even break the chains (*Luke 8:29-33*). Jesus interjected himself into the situation in order to free another human from the literal bonds of evil.

Repeatedly, Jesus faced dangerous situations courageously. For example, one time when Jesus entered the synagogue to teach on the Sabbath, there was a man whose right hand was withered. Jesus knew that the Pharisees and the teachers of the law were scrutinizing his every move to see if he would heal the man on the Sabbath in order that they might find a reason to accuse him of violating the Sabbath laws (*Luke 6:6-7*). Fully aware of their intent, Jesus had the man stand in front of everyone and said to them,

> *"I asked you, which is lawful on the Sabbath: to do good or to do evil, to save life or to destroy it?" He looked around at them all, and then said to the man, "Stretch out your hand." He did so, and his hand was completely restored. But they were furious and began to discuss with one another what they might do to Jesus.* (*Luke 6:9-11*)

Healing the man with the withered hand was a small act compared to Jesus' bold performance in the temple area in Jerusalem only a few days before his death. He drove out those who were buying and selling and overturned the tables of the money changers and the benches of those selling doves, physically stopping anyone from carrying merchandise through the temple courts (*Mark 11:15-16*). In Luke 13:31, some Pharisees warned him,

"Leave this place and go somewhere else. Herod wants to kill you." But Jesus would not back down and told them to

> "Go tell that fox, 'I will drive out demons and heal people today and tomorrow, and on the third day I will reach my goal.' In any case, I must keep going today and tomorrow and the next day—for surely no prophet can die outside Jerusalem!" (Luke 13:32-33)

Even when faced with the threat of Herod's desire to kill him, Jesus exhibited courage as he single-mindedly continued to follow through with his original purpose.

And when the time came for Jesus to prepare himself and his disciples for his crucifixion, he "resolutely set out for Jerusalem. And he sent messengers on ahead, who went into a Samaritan village to get things ready for him" (Luke 9:51-52). Jesus acted bravely in each situation and told others to "Take courage! It is I. Don't be afraid" (Matthew 14:27). Jesus helped his followers reason through their fear as he told them,

> "Do not be afraid of those who kill the body but cannot kill the soul. Rather, be afraid of the One who can destroy both soul and body in hell. Are not two sparrows sold for a penny? Yet not one of them will fall to the ground apart from the will of your Father. And even the very hairs of your head are all numbered. So don't be afraid; you are worth more than many sparrows."
> (Matthew 10:28-31)

As he reasoned through their fear he told each of them to "make up your mind not to worry" (Luke 21:14). Jesus encouraged his followers to cognitively restructure their thoughts so that fear and worry would not debilitate them. Tremendous strength and power result when people are persistent in restructuring their maladaptive cognitions.

Jesus did not lack courage when he undertook many tasks, such as overturning the tables of the money changers, approaching the demon-possessed man who was chained and under guard, and continuing on when the Pharisees warned him that Herod wanted to kill him. Jesus faced each situation courageously. He did not fear what others would do to him. Fear and doubt were not part of his repertoire. "A leader who acknowledges and kowtows to every whim of the sheep/followers is not a leader at all but a non-thinking puppet. Leaders are not to be manipulated by followers pulling their strings."[23] Jesus embraced courage and challenged his followers to do the same (Matthew 14:27).

Courage is an attribute that many leadership scholars have deemed to be a necessary component of an effective leader. Starratt[24] calls for leaders to face opposition courageously. Others also insist that a leader must possess the courage to confront (Hitt,[25] Starratt[26]). Starratt links courage to risk and asserts that a charismatic leader has "courage, a willingness to risk, to risk all in order to achieve the necessary breakthrough in the present circumstances."[27] Leaders must be courageous enough to take big risks, which is exactly what Jesus did. When followers sense a leader's courage, it helps motivate them to join their energies with the leader and draws them toward the vision.[28]

Just as Starratt claims that followers sense the leader's courage, Yukl deduces that self-confidence and strong convictions

> ...increase the likelihood that subordinates will trust the leader's judgment. A leader without confidence in himself or his beliefs is less likely to try to influence people, and when an attempt is made, it is less likely to be successful.[29]

Jesus has been identified as courageous by many scholars (Olson,[30] Jordan,[31] Youssef,[32] Olbricht,[33] Wolff,[34] and Bietz[35]). Wolff points out how Jesus

> ...faced outrageous prejudice, wounded pride and threatened privilege. He persevered in his

vocation, fully aware of the fact that every step he took made the end more certain. Conscious of danger he proceeded in the face of it with calm and firmness. He acted courageously in a threatening situation. Courage to speak boldly, to act vigorously, to proceed regardless of criticism, without ever losing sight of the goal—such courage is vital to leadership.[36]

Jordan[37] also acknowledged the great danger Jesus subjected himself to by continuing to preach and teach in the midst of those who plotted to kill him. Bietz[38] dedicated a whole chapter in his book, *Jesus the Leader*, to discuss how it took great courage for Jesus to overcome many adversities, as did Youssef[39] in *The Leadership Style of Jesus*. In these chapters, Jesus exhorts his followers to not let their heart be troubled and to be of good courage.

Courage

*To encourage means to give heart.
Do you think many people have weak hearts today? If so, why?*

*Who do you know that possesses great moral courage?
How did they obtain that courage?*

*When was the last time you stood up for something even though you knew there would be negative consequences?
What happened?*

Which do you fear more: rejection or demotion? Why?

*What is more important to you: to be liked or to be respected?
Why?*

Persistence

Jesus did not stop spreading his message, even when many rejected and ridiculed him. He was persistent in working for his cause, and proclaimed its importance when he said, "Ask and it will be given to you; seek and you will find; knock and the door will be opened to you. For everyone who asks, receives; he who seeks, finds; and to him who knocks, the door will be opened" (Luke 11:9-10). Persistence requires much hard work. Jesus did not minimize the requirements involved since he had told them to ask, seek, and knock in a continual manner until satisfaction was achieved.

When Jesus was in the vicinity of Tyre, a Greek woman who was born in Syrian Phoenicia came to him. She begged Jesus to drive the demon out of her daughter.

> "First let the children eat all they want," he told her "for it is not right to take the children's bread and toss it to their dogs." "Yes, Lord," she replied, "but even the dogs under the table eat the children's crumbs." Then he told her, "For such a reply, you may go; the demon has left your daughter." She went home and found her child lying on the bed, and the demon gone.
> (Mark 7:27-30)

Jesus honored this woman's persistence and her humble heart.

In Luke 18:2-5, Jesus used a parable to instruct his disciples to be persistent in prayer and effort.

> He said: "In a certain town there was a judge who neither feared God nor cared about men. And there was a widow in that town who kept coming to him with the plea, 'Grant me justice against my adversary.' For some time he refused. But finally he said to himself, 'Even though I don't

fear God or care about men, yet, because this widow keeps bothering me, I will see that she gets justice, so that she won't eventually wear me out with her coming!'"

Through this illustration and others—along with his own life example—it is clear in Jesus' view that persistence is key to influencing others.

Leadership is difficult, and there are many times when leaders come up against tasks that appear to be impossible. Without persistence it is virtually impossible to be an effective leader and move an organization toward its long-term goals. The postmodern leader needs as much persistence as creativity.[40] Blanchard & Peale include persistence in their five principles of ethical behavior. They affirm that "it is especially important to act ethically when it is inconvenient or unpopular to do so.... As Churchill said, 'Never! Never! Never! Never! Give up!'"[41] Jesus is the perfect example of what a postmodern leader should be. Jesus undertook many tasks that seemed insurmountable and continued to boldly surmount them. Again and again, Jesus came across people who rejected him and his message. Undaunted, he kept teaching the truth and persisted in his efforts to lead them to a belief in God—which was expressed as love and compassion for others *(Mark 6:10-13)*.

Covey acknowledges the importance of persistence when working to achieve excellence:

> *Seasoned professionals, however, know that there is simply no shortcut to developing the capability to handle with excellence almost any situation or condition that might occur on the water. Real excellence does not come cheaply. A certain price must be paid in terms of practice, patience, persistence—natural ability notwithstanding.*[42]

To aid in teaching his disciples about persistence, Jesus related to them the parable of the widow who successfully cleared her debt with her adversary before the uncaring judge by being very persistent. Jesus taught his disciples to pray at all times and never give up *(Luke 18:1)*.

Persistence

In what aspect of your life do you most need persistence?
What makes you want to give up?
What makes you want to go on?

How are persistent people generally perceived?

What's the difference between persistence and pushiness?

Describe a time when you benefited from your persistence?

Can people be taught persistence?

How might you create an environment where people want to be persistent?

Plethora of Emotions

$\mathcal{B}$ecause Jesus experienced a wide range of emotions, he was able to have greater empathy for others than if he had blocked out or dismissed particular emotions. No doubt his expressions of empathy were appealing and drew people to him, which allowed others to better relate to him and ultimately enabled him to influence them more effectively. Jesus was in touch with what he was experiencing and acted accordingly. He experienced anger and righteous indignation in Jerusalem when he entered the temple, drove out all who were buying and selling, and overturned the tables of the money changers and those who were selling doves for sacrificial purposes (*Mark 11:15*). This was not a typical behavior for Jesus, but it was appropriate at *that* particular time.

Jesus experienced radical emotions as in Matthew 26:38-39, where his sorrow is evident:

> *"My soul is overwhelmed with sorrow to the point of death. Stay here and watch with me." Going a little farther, he fell with his face to the ground and prayed, "My Father, if it is possible, may this cup be taken from me. Yet not as I will, but as you will."*

Luke 22:44 reveals Jesus' agony: "And being in anguish, he prayed more earnestly, and his sweat was like drops of blood falling to the ground." In Mark 14:33-34 it is recorded that "He took Peter, James and John along with him, and he began to be deeply distressed and troubled 'My soul is overwhelmed with sorrow to the point of death,' he said to them. 'Stay here and keep watch.'" (*Mark 14:34*). Jesus was not exempt from the painful aspects of human existence—nor from those required by his mission.

Thankfulness was one of the positive emotions that Jesus experienced. In Matthew 14:19a, Jesus "directed the people to sit down on the grass. Taking the five loaves and the two fish and looking up to heaven, he gave thanks and broke the loaves."

Jesus could readily access his emotions, which allowed him to have greater empathy for people and thus be better able to meet their needs.

> *Leadership involves both rational and emotional sides of human experience. Leadership includes actions and influences based on reason and logic as well those based on inspiration and passion.... Ignoring either side of human nature would give us an incomplete understanding of leadership.*[43]

As a complement to his rational side, Jesus' plethora of emotions equipped him to relate to others and maximize his leadership potential. Jesus always did the right thing; however, this was not based solely on a rational, linear approach. Jesus allowed himself to fully experience his emotions, no matter how uncomfortable they made him feel. An example of him expressing a painful emotion is documented in the shortest verse in the Bible, when he learned of the death of his friend Lazarus: "Jesus wept" (John 11:35).

Plethora of Emotions

Why are leaders sometimes afraid to express their emotions?

How does the genuine display of emotions allow a leader to more effectively connect with others?

Which is more valuable to you: logic or emotion? Why? Is logic really the opposite of emotion, or is stoicism?

What would be the personal costs if you chose to be an empathetic leader?

Describe how you think Jesus would approach downsizing or a reduction in work force.

Love of Others

Love was the crucial element of Jesus' ministry. Jesus not only taught people to love, but in examining his life, it is evident that he loved and received love from others. He taught that loving God with all of your heart, soul, mind, and strength was the greatest commandment and loving your neighbor as yourself was the second (*Mark 12:30-31*). Jesus declared that "To love [God] with all your heart, with all your understanding and with all your strength, and to love your neighbor as yourself is more important than all burnt offerings and sacrifices" (*Mark 12:33*).

In Matthew 5:44, Jesus offered his followers an enormous challenge: "Love your enemies and pray for those who persecute you." This love went beyond one's comfort zone and had the power to enable significant progress to develop within the leadership relationship. Love was the springboard for Jesus' compassion. Throughout the Scriptures Jesus is noted for having compassion on individuals and groups (*Matthew 9:36 and 20:34; Mark 1:41 and 6:34*).

Unequivocally, love was the premise of Jesus' ministry. For example, When a rich man fell at Jesus' feet and asked how he could inherit eternal life, Jesus looked at him and felt love for him (*Mark 10:21*). Jesus also spoke lovingly of the people in Jerusalem: "...I have longed to gather your children together, as a hen gathers her chicks under her wings, but you were not willing!" (*Luke 13:34*). Finally, Jesus gave the ultimate example of love when he was willing to die for all of mankind on the cross (*John 3:16*).

As with humility, love is not the most commonly addressed issue in the existing leadership literature. Burns recognizes the great power of love and the resultant vulnerability as one becomes, a "slave to the one loved."[44] Jesus was aware of the great power of love, and he loved his followers deeply. This was evident in the way he spoke about them (*Luke 13:34*); the way that he treated them *(Mark 10:21)*; and ultimately by his choice to die for them *(John 3:16)*. The tremendous impact that Jesus had on his followers by loving them should not be overlooked. Surely, his great love for his followers helped convince them to want to be part of this leadership relationship. Covey affirms this point in that

> *...when we love without condition, without strings, we help people feel secure, safe, validated and affirmed in their intrinsic worth, identity and integrity. Their natural growth is encouraged. We make it easy for them to live the laws of life—cooperation, contribution, discipline, integrity—and to discover and to live true to the highest and best within them.... When we violate the primary law of love and start attaching strings and conditions, we actually encourage others to violate the laws of life and become defensive. They may feel they have to prove "I matter" or "I count." They become more concerned defending their "rights" and proving their individuality than they are about honoring their own inner imperatives.*[45]

Apparently, Jesus understood the great role that love would play in influencing his followers and he loved them freely.

Love of Others

Is love a feeling or something else?

Have you ever been loved unconditionally?
If so, how has that influenced you?

If someone told you: "I trust you completely with
all that I have, everyone I love, all that I hold dear"
—what effect would that have on you?

Describe a time when you have seen the love of Jesus
demonstrated by someone in a practical way.

Do you love people because of who they are,
or because of who you are?
What difference does it make?

Would you be able to love others more if you received
more love from others?

Is there anything that is holding you back from
fully embracing the love that has been bestowed on you?

Compassion

$\mathcal{J}$esus' compassionate nature was an asset to his interpersonal relationships. The grace with which he confronted tough issues and hostile situations allowed him to be better received than if he had not been compassionate in his responses. People felt that Jesus understood them and cared about their well-being. Jesus' compassion augmented his ability to influence others, thus producing change. No doubt Jesus' great love for people was at the core of his compassionate heart. In these five separate incidents, the Scriptures point out his compassion.

> • *When he saw the crowds, he had compassion on them, because they were harassed and helpless, like sheep without a shepherd.* (Matthew 9:36)

> • *When Jesus landed and saw a large crowd, he had compassion on them and healed their sick.* (Matthew 14:14)

> • *Jesus had compassion on them and touched their eyes. Immediately they received their sight and followed him.* (Matthew 20:34)

> • *Filled with compassion, Jesus reached out his hand and touched the man. "I am willing [to heal you]," he said. "Be clean!"* (Mark 1:41)

> • *When Jesus landed and saw a large crowd, he had compassion on them, because they were like sheep without a shepherd. So he began teaching them many things.* (Mark 6:34)

As these Scripture demonstrates, Jesus not only felt compassion for people, but he responded to their needs. One example occurred when Jesus had been with a large group of people for three days and refused to send them away hungry. He was finished ministering there and could have left, but instead he had compassion on the people and met their needs (Matthew 15:32). Another display of compassion is the way he responded to children. In Mark 10:14, 16, Jesus asked that the children be permitted to come to him, and then "he took the children in his arms, put his hands on them and blessed them." As children were held in very low esteem in the culture of Jesus' time, this act of compassion is far more significant than the modern reader might recognize.

In addition to acting compassionately, Jesus also taught about it. He related to his followers the parable of the prodigal son, as an example. The father's response to the wayward son in the parable was full of compassion and forgiveness: "But while he [the son] is still a long way off, his father saw him and was filled with compassion for him; he ran to his son, threw his arms around him and kissed him" (Luke 15:20). This is a powerful comparison of a loving, forgiving, compassionate God and an earthly father.

The above parable illustrates that Jesus' compassion was without limits. Even when in dire straits, Jesus was able to show compassion. One of the most striking examples was on the last night of his life when the chief priests, temple guards, and elders arrested him in Gethsemane. Peter, one of Jesus' followers, cut off the ear of the high priest's servant with a sword in a misguided attempt to defend Jesus, but Jesus stopped the defense and reached over and healed the man (Luke 22:50-51). What tremendous compassion he had, even in this desperate moment when his enemies had come to kill him.

As has been shown through the Scriptures, Jesus is noted for having compassion on individuals as well as groups. His compassionate nature was an asset to his interpersonal relationships, and prompted him to lovingly respond to the needs of others. Starratt also suggests that the leader

> ...needs to teach compassion. Compassion does not mean rationalizing or excusing human weakness. It means, rather, the courage to name it, and then forgive it, and then to get on with

the task again. Compassion means the ability to forgive because one knows one's own need for forgiveness.[46]

This is exactly what Jesus did: he did not excuse his followers from falling short; rather, he forgave them. Ray testifies that

> *Of all of the inner qualities that individuals bring to transformation, compassion plays the most central role.... This compassion leads to one recognizing his or her own inner strength and creativity and also seeing that in others. In business this means that people can have the conflict that is necessary for creativity without allowing the conflict to be ad hominem.*[47]

Compassion

What keeps you from seeing the needs of other people?

Why should leaders care about meeting people "where they are"?

Have you ever done something for someone who couldn't repay you? What happened to you as a result?

What is the difference between compassion and being nice?

(Endnotes)

[1] Neill, S.A. (1959). *A Genuinely Human Existence*. New York: Doubleday.

[2] Starratt, R.J. (1993). *The Drama of Leadership*. Washington, D.C.: Falmer Press.

[3] Russell, W.H. (1937). *Christ the Leader*. Milwaukee, WI: Bruce Publishing.

[4] Youssef, M. (1986). *The Leadership Style of Jesus*. Nampa, ID: Victor Books.

[5] Olson, H. (1991). *Power Strategies of Jesus Christ: Principles of Leadership from the Greatest Motivator of All Time*. Tarrytown, New York: Triumph Books.

[6] Covey, S.R. (1989). *Principle-Centered Leadership: Teaching People How to Fish*. Provo, UT: Executive Excellence, p. 100

[7] Hitt, W.D. (1993). *The Model Leader: A Fully Functioning Person*. Columbus, OH: Battelle Press, p. 31

[8] Ibid.

[9] Covey, S.R. (1989). *Principle-Centered Leadership: Teaching People How to Fish*. Provo, UT: Executive Excellence.

[10] Bennis, W. (1989). *On Becoming a Leader*. New York: Addison-Wesley Publishing.

[11] Ibid.

[12] Ibid., p. 3.

[13] Bennis, W. (1989). *On Becoming a Leader*. New York: Addison-Wesley Publishing, p. 3.

[14] Ibid., p. 68

[15] Hitt, W.D. (1993). *The Model Leader: A Fully Functioning Person*. Columbus, OH: Battelle Press.

[16] Renesch, J. (Ed.). (1995). *New Traditions in Business*. San Francisco: Berrett-Koehler, p. 149.

[17] Olson, H. (1991). *Power Strategies of Jesus Christ: Principles of Leadership from the Greatest Motivator of All Time*. Tarrytown, New York: Triumph Books.

[18] Ibid., p. 20.

[19] Covey, S.R. (1990). *The 7 Habits of Highly Effective People*. New York: Simon & Schuster, p. 303.

[20] Ibid., p. 160.

[21] Starratt, R.J. (1993). *The Drama of Leadership*. Washington, D.C.: Falmer Press, p. 108.

[22] Ibid., p. 108.

[23] Drushal (1987). *Attitudes Toward Participative Decision-Making Among Church Leaders: A Comparison of the Influences of Nominal Group Technique, Delphi Survey Technique, and Social Judgment Analysis*. Drushal, Mary E.; Dissertation Abstracts International, Vol. 47 (8-A), Feb 1987, p. 51.

[24] Starratt, R.J. (1993). *The Drama of Leadership*. Washington, D.C.: Falmer Press.

[25] Hitt, W.D. (1993). *The Model Leader: A Fully Functioning Person*. Columbus, OH: Battelle Press.

[26] Starratt, R.J. (1993). *The Drama of Leadership*. Washington, D.C.: Falmer Press.

[27] Ibid., p. 45.

[28] Ibid.

[29] Yukl, G.A. (1981). *Leadership in Organizations*. Englewood Cliffs, NJ: Prentice-Hall, p. 60.

[30] Olson, H. (1991). *Power Strategies of Jesus Christ: Principles of Leadership from the Greatest Motivator of All Time*. Tarrytown, New York: Triumph Books.

[31] Jordan, J.P. (1990). *Secular and Presbyterian Philosophies of Leadership as Compared with the Teaching and Example of Jesus Christ*. Doctoral dissertation, San Francisco Theological Seminary.

[32] Youssef, M. (1986). *The Leadership Style of Jesus*. Wheaton, IL: Victor Books.

[33] Olbricht, T.H. (1979). *The Power To Be*. Fort Worth, TX: Sweet Publishing.

[34] Wolff, R. (1969). *Man at the Top*. Wheaton, IL: Tyndale.

[35] Bietz, R.R. (1980). *Jesus the Leader*. Nampa, ID: Pacific Press.

[36] Wolff, R. (1969). *Man at the Top*. Wheaton, IL: Tyndale, p. 49.

[37] Jordan, J.P. (1990). *Secular and Presbyterian Philosophies of Leadership as Compared with the Teaching and Example of Jesus Christ*. Doctoral dissertation, San Francisco Theological Seminary.

[38] Bietz, R.R. (1980). *Jesus the Leader*. Nampa, ID: Pacific Press.

[39] Youssef, M. (1986). *The Leadership Style of Jesus*. No Wheaton, IL: Victor Books.

[40] Starratt, R.J. (1993). *The Drama of Leadership*. Washington, D.C.: Falmer Press.

[41] Blanchard, K.H. & Peale, N.V. (1988). The Power of Ethical Management. New York: William Morrow & Co., p.63-65.

[42] Covey, S.R. (1989). *Principle-Centered Leadership: Teaching People How to Fish*. Provo, UT: Executive Excellence, p. 277.

[43] Hughes, R.L., Ginnett, R. C., & Curphy, G. J. (1993). *Leadership: Enhancing the Lessons of Experience*. Boston: Irwin, p. 54-55.

[44] Burns, J.M. (1977). *Leadership*. New York: Harper & Row, p. 16.

[45] Covey, S.R. (1989). *Principle-Centered Leadership: Teaching People How to Fish*. Provo, UT: Executive Excellence, p. 143-144.

[46] Starratt, R.J. (1993). *The Drama of Leadership*. Washington, D.C.: Falmer Press, p. 108.

[47] Ray as cited in Renesch, J. (Ed.). (1995). *New Traditions in Business*. San Francisco: Berrett-Koehler, p. 36-37.

2

The Relationship

Between

Jesus and His Followers

Jesus Invested in People

Focused on Few People

Polytrophic Response to People

Modes of Communication

❧

Cultural Climate:

Atmosphere of Openness

Accountability

Fair & Impartial

Symbols to Create Meaning

Celebration

Relationship Between Jesus & His Followers

*I*n addition to Jesus' stellar personal attributes, his dedication to building strong relationships with his followers contributed greatly to his effective leadership. Jesus put people before the product–meeting their spiritual, emotional, and physical needs. Since he focused on fewer numbers of people, Jesus made them feel special and was able to consider their own individual needs when deciding how best to respond to them. Having taken into consideration the situational context and each individual's needs, Jesus' treatment of people was fair and impartial. He also used many modes of communication to better serve his followers.

Jesus provided a meaningful cultural climate that fostered trust within his relationships because he created an open environment that shunned secrecy and embraced the truth. In addition, he provided opportunities for accountability and maintained morale giving meaning to the organization through symbols and celebration.

Jesus' magnificent characteristics influenced the relationships that he had with people. Understanding more about Jesus' relationships provides greater insight into how he enrolled people into a commitment, how he motivated them to continue on, and how he facilitated participation and growth. Jesus' willingness to invest in people is the cornerstone of his relationships.

The picture painted of Jesus' characteristics in the previous section is quite impressive. Jesus was a courageous leader with a clear sense of identity who loved his followers and showed compassion toward them. His highly developed relational skills allowed Jesus to share his emotions with his followers. People knew this gentle, humble, meek, and unselfish man was genuine in his intentions, and were committed to him because he first committed to them.

Jesus Invested in People

Jesus acknowledged the importance of meeting the basic needs of his devotees, which freed them to explore the more complex issues about which he taught. Investing in people's spiritual, physical, and emotional needs. Jesus did not just teach people spiritual truths and then abandon them; he invested totally in their well-being. In Luke 9:10-17, there is a synopsis of Jesus and his followers welcoming the crowd that had followed them, and then providing food for them in the midst of their fatigue. Jesus could have easily sent the people away after he deliverded his message, but he didn't. Even his disciples encouraged Jesus to send the crowd away to find their own food (Mark 6:35-36). In another similar situation Jesus remarked, "I have compassion for these people; they have already been with me three days and have nothing to eat. If I send them home hungry, they will collapse on the way, because some of them have come a long distance" (Mark 8:2-3). Clearly, Jesus was not just interested in the spiritual and emotional well-being of his followers, but he was also concerned about their physical needs.

Jesus invested in people who didn't always appear to be the best and brightest. He chose disciples who many would classify as ordinary and built them up to be great men. Jesus also invested in those that seemed to have no hope. In Luke 8:53-56, there is a story about Jesus healing a girl even though everyone else had given up hope for her survival. The people ridiculed Jesus for trying to heal her.

> They laughed at him, knowing that she was dead. But he took her by the hand and said, "My child, get up!" Her spirit returned, and at once she stood up. Then Jesus told them to give her something to eat. Her parents were astonished, but he ordered them not to tell anyone what had happened.

Jesus continued to amaze people by investing in those that seemed to not have any hope.

Not only did Jesus show his followers how to make wise investments in people by his own actions; he also told his followers where they should make *their* investments.

> *Do not store up for yourselves treasures on earth, where moth and rust destroy, and where thieves break in and steal. But store up for yourselves treasures in heaven, where moth and rust do not destroy, and where thieves do not break in and steal. For where your treasure is, there your heart will be also.* (Matthew 6:19-21)

Jesus encouraged his followers to invest in deeper, more important things than materialism and esoteric pursuits. Jesus also related a parable about a man who invested in two debtors by canceling their debt. (Note: a denarius was a Roman silver coin equal to a day's wage for an ordinary worker.)

> *"Two men owed money to a certain moneylender. One owed him five hundred denarii, and the other fifty. Neither of them had the money to pay him back, so he cancelled the debts of both. Now which of them will love him more?" Simon replied, "I suppose the one who had the bigger debt cancelled." "You have judged correctly," Jesus said.* (Luke 7:41-43)

Through his parables Jesus allows his devotees to see that there are various ways to invest their resources while realizing that the most important resource is another human. The focus within his movement was not on massive political change, monetary wealth, or even popularity, but on the value accorded each individual as a creation of God.

Jesus' investment in others is congruent with Maslow's theory regarding people's hierarchy of needs.[1] Maslow's first category of needs is for physiological satisfaction, which includes primary needs such as sleep, food, and warmth. The second category is the need for safety. This need includes the actual and perceived assurance of safety. The third category is the need for people to give and receive love and to feel like they are a part of a group or community. The fourth level is the need to have esteem and respect for self and others. The final category, which is seldom achieved, is self-actualization. This occurs when someone recognizes and acknowledges their full potential and then develops it. Jesus wanted his followers to grow to reach their full potential, so he helped facilitate this process by challenging them to achieve excellence (Mark 10:17-21).

The key to engaging collaborators into a relationship is by meeting them where they are. If one "challenges people too fast, they will push the authority figure over for failing their expectation for stability. But challenge people too slowly, and they will throw him down when they discover that no progress has been made."[2] Sanford's principles of development also capture this point by claiming that for development to occur optimally, there needs to be an equal amount of challenge and support. If one increases, the other must also increase.[3] Jesus masterfully achieved this balance between challenge and support. Jesus communicated his great expectations for his retinue; however, he also let them know that when they didn't measure up, his grace would be there to fill the gap.

Invested in People

Are you more of a challenging leader, or a supportive one?

How do you know when you have challenged someone too much or too little?

When should you "give up" on someone? Has anyone ever "given up" on you?

Do you manage your human assets with the same attention you give to your financial assets? Why or why not?

What is the origin and definition of the word "invest"?

Focused on Relatively Few People

*I*t is curious that Jesus wanted to reach the whole world yet he focused on so few followers. Jesus did not neglect the masses, but he specifically invested time into a relatively small group of people. He even specialized his efforts within the select group of the 12 apostles. The Gospels tell us that he spent extra time with Peter, James, and John. Coleman comments that Jesus' strategy and hope was

> ...to get men imbued with his life who would [lead the multitudes]. Hence, he concentrated himself upon those who were to be the beginning of this leadership. Though he did what he could to help the multitudes, he had to devote himself primarily to a few men, rather than the masses, in order that the masses could at last be saved. This was the genius of his strategy.[4]

Jesus' plan was to invest much time and energy into a few in order to better implement his vision. Training his disciples was an important focus of his ministry. He took the approach of investing a lot in a few so that this small group could replicate his work. Jesus took the time to be with his disciples and to help them understand the future. On the way to Jerusalem, Jesus explained that he would be betrayed and condemned to death. He also told them about the hope that his resurrection from the grave would provide.

Aside from the Twelve, Jesus commissioned a group of seventy-two others to go out in pairs into every city that he was going to visit (Luke 10:1). Another group he devoted time ministering to was women (Luke 8:1-3), and many of the women in whom Jesus invested became devout followers.

It is noted many times in Scripture that Jesus pulled an inner circle of disciples away for extra training:

◆ Then Jesus went with his disciples to a place called Gethsemane, and he said to them, "Sit here while I go over there and pray." He took Peter and the two sons of Zebedee along with him, and he began to be sorrowful and troubled. (Matthew 26:36-37)

◆ He did not let anyone follow him except Peter, James, and John the brother of James. (Mark 5:37)

◆ As Jesus was sitting on the Mount of Olives opposite the temple, Peter, James, John, and Andrew asked him privately, "Tell us, when will these things happen? And what will be the sign that they are all about to be fulfilled?" (Mark 13:3-4)

Jesus' focus on small groups of people paid off, as he was able to train fewer people more effectively so that his leadership would be better replicated. Just as Jesus focused on small groups of people, he also concerned himself with individuals and their specific needs.

Jesus fully trained his followers in less than three years. His strategy was not to try and meet every person that he possibly could; rather, it was to completely invest himself in a chosen few. This strategy enabled his disciples and those closest to him to have a deeper understanding about how to live abundantly and how to better spread the message that he brought.

Jesus knew that he only had a short time to disciple his followers and that he would have to rely on their ability to carry on with this movement. Hwang's idea that the "leader can only be as good as the followers"[5] is parallel with Jesus' acknowledgment of the importance of investing in his followers to better replicate his leadership. Apparently, this technique of replication served him well since he still has millions of followers two thousand years later.

Focused on Few

List the 12 most important people in your life.

Are you more likely to surround yourself with experts or with teachable individuals? Why?

How did you select these individuals?

How do you systematically invest yourself in these individuals?

Why do leaders often feel compelled to dramatically influence large numbers of people?

Polytrophic Response to People

The word *polytrophic* is derived from the Greek words *poly*, meaning "many," and *trophos*, meaning "to nourish"; hence "to nourish in many ways."[6] The concept of polytrophism can be traced back to the days of antiquity. In a Homeric commentary, Pythagoras and Antisthenes discussed the flexible influence of polytrophism.

> Antisthenes said that Homer did not praise Odysseus more than he blamed him; he called him much-turning, many-sided, many-faceted, versatile, shifty, changeful, complicated, complex.... Wherefore, Homer says that Odysseus, wise and good as he is, is polytrophic, complex, just because he knows how to communicate with people by means of many modes. So also Pythagoras is said to have composed, when requested to make speeches addressed to children, childlike discourses; and with the same speeches addressed to rulers magisterial arguments, and to young men arguments appropriate to them. For the mode of wisdom, befitting each class it is the part of wisdom to search out; and it is the part of naiveté to address a single kind of statement to different classes of people.[7]

Not only did Greek culture contribute to the understanding of polytrophic leadership, but also, during the days of Jesus, the concept was enhanced through the emerging Judeo-Christian culture. Baird cites the New Testament as the "foremost contribution to the concept [of polytrophic leadership].... As soon as one begins to examine in earnest the recorded actions of Christ, they cannot help being struck by his extraordinarily varied approach in dealing with different people."[8]

Baird[9] conceptualized a model of polytrophic leadership built upon the assumption that all individuals have the ability to become self-actualized, but need to be guided through the process. The leader meets the followers where each is at, seeking to bring maturity to those who are immature. The continuum spans from the autocratic leader—who best engages the dependent and inexperienced person—to the participative leader—who is able to empower the mature and self-actualized person to share in the leadership responsibility. Covey maintains that when

> ...you have little confidence in a person, make the desired results very clear, measurable, and quantifiable; establish stringent guidelines; [specify] resources; have frequent progress reports; and make sure consequences soon follow the behavior. If you have great confidence in a person, involve him in setting the performance criteria and then allow him to evaluate himself. In their hearts, people know how they're doing, but if the trust level is low, they will not be honest with themselves or others. The performance appraisal then becomes a meaningless game.[10]

Polytrophic leadership does not simply adapt a style of leadership to fit a particular situation. Maslow wrote that the follower's entire well-being should be taken into consideration, and the process of leadership should attempt to foster an experience that moves the individual toward "the full use and exploitation of talent, capacities, potentialities, etc. Such people seem to be fulfilling themselves and doing the best that they are capable of doing."[11] After the polytrophic leadership experience is discontinued, the follower has not only participated in the leadership process but has grown to a deeper level of maturity interpersonally. In the next leadership experience he should be able to partake in a greater, shared leadership relationship.

At the heart of the successs of a polytrophic leader is a basic sense of trust that is cultivated between the leader and followers. This trust is fostered by the genuineness of the leader's personality and actions, and the fact that he is open to his followers. Baird describes a polytrophic leader as someone who has

...proof of solid character, goodwill, and competence as constituted by the judgments others make of him.... The trust that cements polytrophic leadership is born not only of "what" but "how," as well. The polytrophic leader is magnificent in his ability to lead by example.[12]

The congruence of the leader internalizing her/his values, and then using them as a base to pursue the shared vision provides a solid example to the followers.

The polytrophic leader seeks to meet the needs of the follower by discovering his/her unique individual differences. "What finer realization exists than the tremendously satisfying acknowledgment that in our uniqueness there is profound worth, and beyond that worth the possibility of utility for the benefit of the world."[13]

In the pursuit of helping others move toward self-actualization, "the beauty of such a facilitated process lies in the realization that those caught up in the ongoing activities are challenged, but never coerced; motivated, but not manipulated; loved, but not used."[14] The polytrophic leader is further characterized by Baird with the following attributes:

He is capable of working the entire range of the leadership continuum as a function of his concern for the individual. He handles with congruency and candor the spectrum of values and tacit norms of those individuals and organizations with which he is involved. He utilizes the full range of paralleling techniques of each role on the continuum to facilitate individual growth toward maturity, rather than for mere control of subordinates. He has learned through experience in a diversity of situations the skills of making good choices in terms of interpersonal relationships, trust development, risk-taking, the propitious use of language, and values exchange.[15]

The concern for the individual's growth is a top priority. The polytrophic model considers the individual's development and helps guide the leader in choosing a particular manner in which to serve the follower.

Owyoung in his thesis *A Biblical Evaluation of Secular Leadership Styles in Light of the Ministry of Jesus Christ as Servant Leader*, evaluated five secular leadership styles. The styles considered include: bureaucratic, permissive, laissez faire, participative, and autocratic. After comparing each of these styles to that of Jesus, Owyoung found that no particular category could be identified as Jesus' sole leadership style. Owyoung concluded that each style had strengths and weaknesses and that each one may benefit an organization.[16] Owyoung's finding reinforced polytrophism's premise that there is not one particular style of leadership that a leader should adopt. Polytrophism's holistic view of the individual takes into consideration the individual's personal growth and seeks to aid in their development just as transformational leadership does.

Jesus responded to people in different ways. One assumption that may be derived from his unique approach to people is that he reacted to each person according to their heart motives, and their capability to comprehend the lesson. With people who had good motives and wanted to learn, he used reason. For example, in Luke 8:5-8, he took time to explain what the parable of the sown seeds meant to his disciples who had earnest hearts. He even explained his actions to some of the Pharisees, as in Mark 2:18-20, when he explained why his disciples did not fast. He informs the Pharisees that after he is gone, "on that day they will fast."

At other times Jesus remained silent to accusation, especially when the person was going to condemn him no matter what he said *(Matthew 26:62-63)*. As part of this rationale, Jesus also cautioned in Matthew 7:6, "Do not give dogs what is sacred; do not throw your pearls to pigs. If you do, they may trample them under their feet, and then turn and tear you to pieces." He suggests employing discretion and wisdom in one's response to others.

Jesus valued people as beings worthy of dignity, and therefore did not ridicule his followers when they were in error. He treated them with respect, and this is evident in the response Jesus had to John and James' request to sit at his right and left side in his glory (Mark 10:37-40). He could have scolded them for being selfish and egotistical; but instead, he gave a lesson on the meaning of true greatness, which is servanthood (Mark 10:43-45).

We can again witness this in Jesus' compassionate response to the woman brought before him to be stoned on charges of adultery. He went so far as to kneel before her as he pardoned her and treated her warmly and gently, telling her that he did not condemn her and to leave her life of sin (John 8:11).

But Jesus knew that others would not understand a warm and gentle admonition from him, so he responded to them in a more appropriate manner. The moneychangers and the dove sellers in the temple could only understand a physical response, so Jesus "overturned the tables of the moneychangers and the benches of those selling doves, and would not allow anyone to carry merchandise through the temple courts" (Mark 11:15-16). All these responses to people were adapted to—and appropriate for—the needs of the situation.

Polytrophic Response

Do you think it's better to be consistent or flexible?
Are these concepts mutually exclusive?

Is it desirable to be all things to all people? Why or why not?

Some leaders sell their ideas, but many leaders feel compelled to
bribe people into action with rewards or payments.
Some leaders tell people what to do, while others like to
gel and participate with their people.
Which approach do you practice the most? Why?
Which approach do you practice the least? Why?

Have you known a wise person?
How did you know they were wise?
How did they acquire their wisdom?

How can you learn to discern the motives of other people?

Modes of Communication

A facet of Jesus' polytrophic response to people is seen through his use of many different modes of communication. His adversaries attempted to verbally entrap him within the rules and regulations of their religious practices. But Jesus had communicated so magnificently that "they were unable to trap him in what he had said there in public. And astonished by his answer, they became silent" (Luke 20:26). Jesus used cleverly worded questions to deflect criticism; as in Luke 6:9, when he said to the scribes and the Pharisees, "I ask you, which is lawful on the Sabbath: to do good or to do evil, to save life or to destroy it?" Even though their law said it was unlawful to "work" on the Sabbath, they were logically trapped by Jesus' answer/question.

Another example deals with Jesus healing on the Sabbath as recorded in Luke 14:1-6. He wanted to heal a man on the day of rest, but knew that if he did he would be scrutinized. So he set up the situation by asking the Pharisees and the experts in the law whether or not it was lawful to heal on the Sabbath. They responsed with silence, and Jesus proceeded to heal the man. He then asked who among them would not rescue a child or ox that had fallen into a well on the Sabbath, and they *still* had nothing to say.

As can be seen in the above examples, Jesus often used the technique of answering questions with questions. In Jerusalem, when some Pharisees and teachers of the law asked Jesus why his disciples broke the tradition of washing their hands before they ate, Jesus came right back with a question: "And why do you break the command of God for the sake of your tradition?" (Matthew 15:3). In Luke 20:39, even some of the teachers of the law acknowledged his savvy communication when they affirmed, "Well said, teacher!"

Another mode of communication was the utilization of parables to do much of his teaching (Mark 4:2). Jesus chose parables that people could relate to, like a farmer sowing seeds to depict the reactions people have to hearing the gospel (*Matthew 13:3-8*). Jesus used visual parables, such as one that proposed the adoption of a new way of thinking: "No one tears a patch from a new garment and sews it on an old one. If he does, he will have torn the new garment, and the patch from the new will not match the old" (*Luke 5:36*). He reiterated that illustration with another parable that cautioned against using new wine in old wineskins (*Luke 5:37-39*). He also used stories like that of the Good Samaritan (*Luke 10:30-37*) to answer questions directed at him such as, "Who is my neighbor?"

Similes were a favorite mode of communication for Jesus. In Matthew 13:47-48, heaven is compared to a fishing net, from which the bad fish are discarded. Sometimes Jesus provided more than words and utilized live visuals, as in Matthew 18:2-4:

> *He called a little child and had him stand among them. And he said: "I tell you the truth, unless you change and become like little children, you will never enter the kingdom of heaven. Therefore, whoever humbles himself like this child is the greatest in the kingdom of heaven."*

Jesus knew the impact of such communication was powerful.

At other times he used physical symbols to communicate meaning as in Mark 14:22-24, where bread and wine became symbolic of Jesus' bodily sacrifice.

> *While they were eating, Jesus took bread, gave thanks and broke it, and gave it to his disciples, saying, "Take it; this is my body." Then he took the cup, gave thanks and offered it to them, and they all drank from it. "This is my blood of the covenant, which is poured out for many."*

Another technique Jesus utilized in communicating was choosing language that appealed to others' senses in a multi-experiential way. Words such as "being shown," "filled," "called," "comforted," "given," etc., were spoken in an artful way to reframe a situation and bring hope to those who were in discouraging circumstances. In the Sermon on the Mount, the Beatitudes—which begin with "blessed are..." terminology—convey hope for a brighter future to those who are suffering in one way or another *(Matthew 5:3-11)*.

Within the theme of respect for others, Jesus sometimes chose to confront indirectly. Many times he would speak about a subject without pointing his finger at anyone and leave it to the ones who were convicted to understand and embrace the correction. This is exemplified in Luke 14:7, when Jesus noticed how the guests had been picking out the places of honor at the table. In response, he told them a parable about the rewards of humility.

Yet at other times, he communicated boldly and unabashedly. When Jesus was told that his truth was insulting, he furthered his admonition with the comment, "And you experts in the law, woe to you, because you load people down with burdens they can hardly carry, and you yourselves will not lift one finger to help them" *(Luke 11:45-46)*. Jesus did not mince words when the circumstances justified a strong response.

Still at other times his response was direct, but not harsh. He spoke to people and acknowledged their weaknesses and challenged them to a higher standard. In Mark 14:38, he told them, "Watch and pray so that you will not fall into temptation. The spirit is willing, but the body is weak." Jesus did not kowtow to what people wanted to hear, as shown in Matthew 9:4: "Knowing their thoughts, Jesus said, 'Why do you entertain evil thoughts in your hearts?'"

Jesus had a varied communication style: at times he encouraged *(Matthew 5:14-16)* and at other times he rebuked *(Mark 16:14)*, warned sternly *(Matthew 9:30)*, or confronted directly *(Luke 22:48)* as when Jesus confronted Judas directly and asked him, "Judas, are you betraying the Son of Man with a kiss?"

In another incident, Jesus spoke directly and confronted the Pharisees' and Herodians' plan to entrap him in one of his own statements. When they asked Jesus whether or not they should pay taxes to Caesar, Jesus knew their hypocrisy and said, "Why are you trying to trap me?" *(Mark 12: 14-16)*. But after his betrayal and arrest when he was on trial for his life before the Sanhedrin, Jesus shocked his audience by remaining silent throughout the questioning by the high priest *(Matthew 26:62-63)*.

For the most part, Jesus utilized his brilliant rhetoric to turn situations around. Yet he wasn't all talk, when the time came to take action, as seen in the previously mentioned example of expelling the moneychangers from the temple courts *(Matthew 21:12-13)*. Jesus had the courage to stand up to his adversaries, and his utilization of many modes of communication added great strength to his ability to practice leadership successfully.

Jesus took into consideration the individuals–or audience–that he was addressing when choosing the mode and style of his communication. Starratt points out the need for a leader to communicate in a way that adopts the other person's role or perspective.[17] He suggests the following questions to consider when communicating:

> *What choice of vocabulary will carry the message best? What references to others' probable experiences would serve as examples for his message? What allusion to people whom the other might consider credible authorities would add weight to his message? In conveying the message, the actor chooses words and imagery which he thinks will make an impression on the other. In the process of conveying the message, the actor watches the other carefully for cues as to whether his message is getting across and whether the other is suitably impressed.[18]*

Jesus skated through difficult situations because of his highly developed reasoning and communication skills. He varied his communication style depending on the people he was addressing and adapted it for each situation. At times Jesus communicated directly (Matthew 9:4), indirectly (Luke 14:7), boldly (Luke 11:45-47), sternly (Matthew 9:30), encouragingly (Matthew 5:3-12), cleverly (Luke 20:26), rhetorically (Luke 20:27-40), and silently (Matthew 26:62-63).

Bergquist explains that the medium used to convey the message makes a difference.[19] Jesus used stories (Luke 10:30-37), parables (Mark 4:2), and similes (Matthew 13:47-48) to aid in his teaching, and the language he used was multi-experiential. In addition to his verbal communication, he used visuals (Matthew 18:2-4) and symbols (Mark 14:22-25) to create deeper meaning in his communication. Jesus' stellar communication ability was reinforced by his actions. The authenticity in his leadership through example added to the great strength and believability of his message.

Multi-Modal Communication

Which mode of communication do you utilize primarily—visual, auditory, or hands-on? Why?

Do you prefer sophisticated or more informal channels of communication?

Describe a time when you had to try several different methods in order to successfully communicate the message. What were the results?

How might the phrase "new wine in old wineskins" relate to your approach to communicating information today?

How might you develop and use analogies and metaphors for more effective communication?

Describe a time when you told a story to illustrate an idea. Was it effective?

Cultural Climate

The strong, well-maintained cultural climate that Jesus wove together among his disciples and other followers provided a solid foundation for him to practice extraordinary leadership. Jesus paid great attention to maintaining morale and keeping an open atmosphere, and provided opportunities for accountability, celebration, and symbols to create meaning in his organization.

In addition to creating a unified climate, Jesus let his disciples know their importance. One example was when the 12 apostles stood with him during a sermon after he had chosen them. This might be likened to an installation of officers. Luke 6:17 records that Jesus "went down with them and stood on a level place. A large crowd of his disciples was there and a great number of people from all over Judea, from Jerusalem, and from the coast of Tyre and Sidon." Jesus used this public affirmation to share with his disciples his desire for them to be with him. In Luke 22:15, he said to them, "I have eagerly desired to eat this Passover with you before I suffer."

Jesus created a learning environment where there was a willingness to hear and to learn. When Jesus informed Simon that he had some information for him, Simon instantly replied, "Tell me, teacher" (Luke 7:40). This illustrates that Jesus' followers were teachable and eager to learn. The disciples' desire to learn is evident in Luke 11:1: "...one of his disciples said to him, 'Lord, teach us to pray, just as John taught his disciples.'" Jesus fulfilled their desire to learn when he invested time and effort in teaching his disciples, especially in the area of prayer (Matthew 6: 5-13).

Jesus communicated his experiences with his disciples, and acknowledged their value to the organization in order to help build a close cultural climate. For example, in Mark 14:3, when Jesus was dining with Simon the Leper in Bethany, a woman poured very expensive perfume on Jesus' feet. In Mark 14:9, it is noted that Jesus said, "I tell you the truth, wherever the gospel is preached throughout the world, what she has done will also be told, in memory of her." Jesus used acknowledgement of a person's love and sacrifice to strengthen the cultural climate and maintain morale among followers.

Starratt affirms that the "involvement with the cultural aspects of the organization is the most important task of the leader."[20] Jesus created an open environment that was fair and impartial. He used symbols, accountability, and celebration to create a close cultural climate that was unified.

Maintaining morale within his band of disciples was important to Jesus. The "organizational climate is related to how well organizational members get along with each other."[21] When Jesus' disciples became agitated with one another, Jesus stepped in and brought unity by diffusing their anger (Mark 10: 41-45). Channon asserts that

> The challenge for business leaders in the 21st century is to assume the mantle of spiritual elder for their cultures, so that life doesn't become trivial and gray for all the people who spend most of their life at work. Corporations are our new communities.[22]

Jesus provided an environment where his followers could find meaning through learning.

According to Psalmonds Jesus created an environment for his followers where they could feel a sense of satisfaction.[23] People "felt free to go to him and tell him what he should do, and they assumed Jesus would do what in fact they had suggested."[24] Jesus heightened morale through celebration. By focusing on others' needs and calming their fears through his presence, Jesus provided relief from tension and fatigue, and maintained contact between himself and his followers and members of the larger group.

Jesus brought unity to his team of disciples. When James and John requested to sit in the seats of honor in heaven, the disciples were outraged at the brothers' audacity, while probably secretly wishing they had asked first. In order to unify this team of competitive members and take the opportunity to teach them, Jesus called the disciples together and told them how they were different than those who were regarded as the rulers of the Gentiles who lorded their power over their subjects. Rather, the disciples were instructed that "...whoever wants to become great among you must be your servant, and whoever wants to be first must be slave of all. For even the Son of Man did not come to be served, but to serve, and to give his life as a ransom for many" (Mark 10:42-45). Again, at the Passover dinner, the disciples disputed about who was going to be considered the greatest. Jesus did not name anyone or point any fingers. He simply and eloquently reminded them that the kings of the Gentiles who exercise authority over the people call themselves Benefactors. "But you are not to be like that. Instead, the greatest among you should be like the youngest, and the one who rules like the one who serves. For who is greater, the one who is at the table or the one who serves? Is it not the one who is at the table? But I am among you as one who serves" (Luke 22:26-27). Maintaining morale brought unity to the group and encouraged an atmosphere of trust and openness.

Fortune magazine exhorts businesses to "forget your tired old ideas about leadership. The most successful corporation...will be something called a learning organization."[25] Senge has declared that "the organizations that will truly excel in the future will be the organizations that discover how to tap people's commitment and capacity to learn at all levels in an organization."[26] The key to success is learning faster than your competitor, which includes learning at each level. Jesus facilitated learning in his organization through teaching with parables, stories, and by the example of his transparent life.

Cultural Climate

How well do the people you work with know you?
How well do you know them?

How do you help people find meaning in their work?

How do you know when learning is occurring in your workplace?

How do you know if that learning is valuable
and consistent with the intended goal?

Have you observed committed leaders who were not able to foster
that same level of commitment throughout an organization?
Why do you think this happens?

Should leaders be honest and openly express when their own
spirit is deflated and depleted? Why or why not?

Why is the root word of morale, "moral"?

How do you support and acknowledge the energies and
accomplishments of others?

What do you do when your own morale is flagging?

How did Jesus respond to the fears and anxieties
of those around him? How do you?

Atmosphere of Openness

*T*he cultural climate that Jesus advocated was one of openness, completely embraced by the truth. Jesus spoke candidly to his followers about the risks and sacrifices involved in participating in leadership with him.

> *You will be betrayed even by parents, brothers, relatives and friends, and they will put some of you to death. All men will hate you because of me. But not a hair of your head will perish. By standing firm you will gain life.* (Luke 21:16-19)

Jesus compares this openness to light exposing darkness. In Luke 8:16-17, Jesus gave them a visual illustration to understand this concept:

> *No one lights a lamp and hides it in a jar or puts it under a bed. Instead, he puts it on a stand, so that those who come in can see the light. For there is nothing hidden that will not be disclosed, and nothing concealed that will not be known or brought out into the open.*

Jesus' followers learned to trust him in this open environment. This is illustrated in Luke 5:5-7 when Simon, a professional fisherman, did what Jesus told him to do with the fishing nets even though he thought it ridiculous. No doubt the atmosphere of openness had helped facilitate trust for Simon because he did exactly what Jesus advised. Simon said

> *"Master, we've worked hard all night and haven't caught anything. But because you say so, I will let down the nets." When they had done so, they caught such a large number of fish that their nets began to break. So they signaled their partners in the other boat to come and help them, and they came and*

filled both boats so full that they began to sink.
(Luke 5:5-7)

Surely Simon was astonished at this event, which must have engendered a deeper sense of trust in Jesus.

In this atmosphere of openness Jesus spoke honestly and did not mince words. Just as light exposes darkness, so does the spoken word reveal the status of one's heart. Jesus reveals this truth to the Pharisees in Matthew 12:34-37, when he tells them,

> *You brood of vipers, how can you who are evil say anything good? For out of the overflow of the heart the mouth speaks. The good man brings good things out of the good stored up in him, and the evil man brings evil things out of the evil stored up in him. But I tell you that men will have to give account on the day of judgment for every careless word they have spoken. For by your words you will be acquitted, and by your words you will be condemned.*

This passage reveals the importance of words and the inevitability of being held accountable for what one speaks.

Jesus' organization was based on openness and truthfulness. He cleaved to the truth in all his interactions. In the organizational leadership literature there is much talk about the need to have an open organization. An open organization supports truth, freedom, empowerment, justice, and collaboration. Untruth would then be diametrically opposed to an open organization, and would foster mistrust.[27] Nair elaborates by saying, "Secrecy is the enemy of trust and is responsible for much of the distrust that exists between business and society, corporations and customers, management and employees."[28]

Jesus undeniably spoke candidly to his followers about risk and sacrifice, and the picture he painted for them was anything but glossy. Nair reinforces this principle by examining the antithesis of openness: "If those who seek openness do not meet their commitment to be truthful, they are equally responsible for the cycle of deception by providing those who have the information the justification for secrecy."[29] Heifetz adds to this idea by claiming that an organization is only as sick as it is secretive.[30] Truthfulness, openness, and trust were powerful components in the relationships that Jesus cultivated with his followers.

Open Atmosphere

What's the connection between openness and standing firm?

Should leaders be open to everything? Why or why not?

What importance do you place on the words you speak?

What are the effects of gossip and the "grapevine" on an atmosphere of openness?

Describe a time when you gave a co-worker your trust. What was the result?

What is the relationship between trust and openness?

How can you know whom and when to trust?

Accountability

The lack of secrecy in Jesus' organization fostered accountability among his followers—a natural extension of this open environment. The Scriptures report that the group was in the habit of meeting and debriefing. It is noted that, "When the apostles returned, they reported to Jesus what they had done. Then he took them with him and they withdrew by themselves to a town called Bethsaida" (Luke 9:10). Jesus held others accountable through this practice. He emphasized this point through his usual pattern of storytelling. Jesus told his disciples: "There was a rich man whose manager was accused of wasting his possessions. So he called him in and asked him, 'What is this I hear about you? Give an account of your management, because you cannot be manager any longer'" (Luke 16:1-2). Accountability is woven tightly together with openness and trust. Together, they enhance the cultural climate and provide a foundation from which to seek meaning.

Accountability naturally blossoms within an organization that has an atmosphere of openness. When there is nothing to hide in an organization, accountability may be viewed to be less threatening. Another way to reduce anxiety associated with accountability is through Covey's model[31] of win/win accountability where people evaluate themselves based on the criteria that they helped to construct. Accountability is reciprocal in that not only are the followers accountable to the leaders, but leaders are accountable to the followers. "A leader is responsible for the organization itself. As its chief representative, the leader is held accountable and responsible for the welfare and the actions of the organization."[32]

Jesus employed the principle of accountability with his apostles, as in Luke 9:10 when they returned from their missionary internships. Throughout his ministry Jesus always put the welfare and growth of the followers above the task at hand. In addition, Jesus lived by a single standard of conduct, which fostered trust from the followers and encouraged accountability.

Nair challenges people to "make a commitment to live by a single standard of conduct—for if we do our leaders will have to follow."[33] It is much easier to hold others accountable if we are measuring up to the moral standards ourselves.

Accountability

Who are you accountable to?

As you develop and obtain greater influence as a leader,
for what purpose(s) will you use your gifts?

What is the most difficult question
someone could ask you and why?

What do you think is the origin and meaning of the word
"privilege"?

Is there any relationship between accountability and privilege?

What are the implications of the following statement: "To whom much has been given, much shall be required?"

Fair and Impartial

Jesus treated people respectfully and without prejudice. He believed in diversity and broke many social taboos of the day when he dined with sinners (Luke 5:29-30), invested time in women and included them in his ministry (Luke 8:1-3), and spent time blessing children (Matthew 19:13-14). In Luke 5:29-32 there is a dialogue which confirms that the Pharisees and the teachers of the law were not happy that Jesus was spending time with people of such low moral character. They complained to his disciples, "Why do you eat and drink with tax collectors and 'sinners'?" Jesus answered them, "It is not the healthy who need a doctor, but the sick. I have not come to call the righteous, but sinners to repentance." Jesus was not concerned with the social status of those to whom he ministered; rather, he used the social custom of sharing a meal as a form of outreach.

It is worthy to note the type of people with whom Jesus dined, as these were specific people to whom he had reached out. When he called out to Zacchaeus (the despised chief tax collector for the city of Jericho), and said, "Come down, I must stay at your house today," the little man, who had been sitting in a sycamore tree because of his small stature, had an immediate response—he came down at once. This did not sit well with the surrounding crowd, which noted that Jesus had "gone to be the guest of a 'sinner'" (Luke 19:5-7). Additionally, Jesus did not practice reverse discrimination; he also accepted an invitation to dine at a Pharisee's house (Luke 7:36).

In addition to spending time with the "sinners" in society, Jesus treated women with care and respect, and included them in his ministry. At the time, women were another group of people with little or no social power, yet they were a pivotal force in his work, especially financially. Luke 8:1-3 relates that many women—three are mentioned by name—helped "to support Jesus and his disciples out of their own means." Women were also given importance through Jesus' presence. After his resurrection, Jesus chose to appear first to women, as cited in

Matthew 28:8-10. Once the shock of his appearance wore off, the women were told to "Go and tell my brothers to go to Galilee; there they will see me." Jesus continually used those held in low esteem in Judaic culture to participate in significant acts. This type of fair and impartial behavior had earned Jesus a reputation that even those who were against him couldn't deny.

In fact, he was so well-known for being impartial that even spies acknowledged his impartiality. In Luke 20:21, it is recorded that these infiltrators admitted to Jesus: "Teacher we know that you speak and teach what is right, and...do not show partiality but teach the way of God in accordance with the truth...." This treatment extended to his family members also. He did not give his brother or mother special treatment or invite them to go ahead of all the other people who were trying to see him (Mark 3:32-35).

Part of Jesus' concept of fair and impartial behavior included acts of kindness without remuneration. In Luke 14:13-14, Jesus asserted, "...when you give a banquet, invite the poor, the crippled, the lame, the blind, and you will be blessed. Although they cannot repay you, you will be repaid at the resurrection of the righteous." In Matthew 20:1-16, he tells the parable of the landowner who hired workers at different times of the day and then paid them all the same amount for their labor. The point of this parable is to teach people not to compare their blessings with others'. Jesus always treated people impartially; however, that did not mean that he treated them in the same way.

In Jesus' quest to change the status quo, he broke many social norms in establishing a cultural climate that valued diversity and treated people fairly and impartially. One of the most noticeable ways in which he crossed these social boundaries was by investing in women, children, and minorities. The dominant culture criticized Jesus' inclusive responses to people. But Jesus was impartial; he dined not only with the sinners, tax collectors, and prostitutes, but also with the self-righteous Pharisees.

Starratt's call for leadership in the postmodern world is congruent with Jesus' inclusive nature. He calls for leadership that is

> ...able to critique the shortcomings [of], and the myths that support, the status quo. It has to be a leadership grounded in a new anthropology, an understanding of the human condition as both feminine and masculine, as multicultural, as both crazy and heroic, violent and saintly, and as embedded in and therefore responsible to nature. We are talking of a leadership broadly based throughout society, rather than a leadership exercised by a select few.[34]

This call for new postmodern leadership is parallel to what Jesus was practicing 2000 years ago. Jesus' leadership was based on interdependence (which will be discussed later) and equality.

Hwang coined the word "other-esteem," which is based on the equality of people. Other-esteem is "the respect, acceptance, caring, valuing and promoting of others, who may think, feel, and act differently."[35] Individualism is revered in the American culture; yet, it takes far greater strength and courage to realize and accept interaction with and dependency on others.[36]

Leadership scholars and practitioners are faced with the issues of inclusion and integration. The metaphor of the melting pot is being replaced by the salad—a place where people do not have to give up their identity to be a harmonious contributor. Cynthia Barnum maps out three steps for gaining a global perspective. The first imperative is "knowing thyself." Understanding your own cultural conditioning and biases serves as a base from which to understand others. The next step is to understand another culture and how it is similar to and different from your own. The final step is to conceptualize the larger picture of how the different cultures might fit together.[37]

Fair & Impartial

How would you describe most of your friends?
Are they more like you than different?

What type of a person would you prefer to not have as a friend?
Why?

Describe a time when you acted fairly and impartially even
though it was unpopular. Did you anticipate anything in return?
What was the outcome?

How can you become a leader who can talk with anybody
and learn from everybody?

Do you think most people act fairly? If not, why don't they?

Symbols to Create Meaning

Jesus knew the importance of symbols for creating a cultural climate in which people would want to be a part. The symbolic act of baptism is key in Jesus' movement. Jesus did not *need* to be baptized, but he participated in it to show what an important symbol it is *(Mark 1:9)*. Another symbol that Jesus used was the taking of communion. In Matthew 26:26-28, it is cited that

> While they were eating, Jesus took bread, gave thanks and broke it, and gave it to his disciples, saying, "Take and eat; this is my body." Then he took the cup, gave thanks and offered it to them, saying, "Drink from it, all of you. This is my blood of the covenant, which is poured out for many for the forgiveness of sins."

When they had finished, Jesus concluded with a hymn and they set out for the Mount of Olives. These symbols helped people to better understand the concepts that Jesus was trying to teach and served to create deeper meaning in their beliefs.

Starratt deduces that symbols are very important and can be manifested as "words, literary allusions, gestures, bodily posture, clothing, name dropping, artifacts associated with oneself, etc. The appropriate use of symbols reveals what one thinks of oneself and what one thinks of the other."[38] Symbols can be manifested in many different ways. At the Last Supper, Jesus used bread and a cup of wine to symbolize his body and blood, which would be shed the next day through his death for sin. To create a vision for the future, Jesus added that he would not drink the wine again until the day that they are united together in heaven. Bennis and Nanus affirm this gesture, as they include symbolism as one of their major themes to communicate vision.[39] Starratt also claims that because people are searching for meaning in life they turn to symbols to find it.[40] Jesus used symbols such as baptism and communion to provide meaning in their quest toward developing community.

Symbols to Create Meaning

List three to five powerful symbols in your home or work life.

Describe a time when you successfully used a symbol
to convey an idea.

If a co-worker were to use a symbol to depict your leadership
approach, what would they choose and why?

What do roads, rivers, and runways symbolize?
What do mountains, meadows, and midwives symbolize?
Could you use any of these metaphors to effectively
communicate an idea? How?

Jesus' Relationships

Celebration

Jesus recognized the value of celebration in people's quest to find meaning. He was far from being a party-pooper. Jesus consistently accepted many dinner and banquet invitations. In fact, Jesus' first miracle was at a marriage celebration. One of the most famous celebrations in history—which artists have painted and poets pontificated about—was the "Last Supper," where Jesus and his disciples celebrated Passover. Luke 22:14-16 informs us that Jesus shared the importance of this last Passover with the apostles before his crucifixion: "And he said to them, I have eagerly desired to eat this Passover with you before I suffer. For I tell you, I will not eat it again until it finds fulfillment in the kingdom of God."

Celebration was not only for the benefit of his group; it also affected Jesus deeply. Food was a focal point of many celebrations. Jesus hosted two alfresco dinner parties—one with over four thousand people, and one with five thousand. Jones points out that the "night before he was arrested, he gathered his staff together to sing songs and dine. When crowds came, Jesus was adamant that nobody leaves with an empty stomach. He always managed to locate food for them."[41] By focusing on others' needs and calming their fears through his presence, Jesus provided relief from tension and fatigue and maintained contact between himself and his followers, and members of the group.

In another example, in Matthew 21:7-8, Jesus rides a donkey into Jerusalem in a parade-like manner over cloaks and palm branches that had been laid down and spread in the road for him by the multitudes. And Matthew 21:9-10 records that

> The crowds that went ahead of him and those that followed shouted, "Hosanna to the Son of David!" "Blessed is he who comes in the name of the Lord!" "Hosanna in the highest!" When Jesus entered Jerusalem, the whole city was stirred and asked, "Who is this?"

This was a fantastic celebration in which Jesus participated, and it is still honored today as Palm Sunday. This gave his followers an opportunity to celebrate his arrival.

Celebration is an important aspect of an organization's culture. Deforest claims that "celebration is tied to the very fabric of corporate culture. The more celebration is woven into the workplace, the more its results can be measured in direct productivity, profit, and people."[42] Bryson and Crosby affirm, "Celebrations are important ways of recognizing progress toward or achievement of organizational goals. Celebration should emphasize key organizational values, be public, and have personal involvement of leaders."[43] There is a new trend that is catching on in corporate America, one that emphasizes *meaning* in the culture. Starratt adds,

> *Leadership in the cultural perspective is exercised not so much by scientific management as by guarding essential values of the culture, by reminding people in the organization of the essential meanings of the culture, by promoting rituals and celebrations which sustain those essential meanings and values of the organization.*[44]

One way that Jesus provided meaning for his organization was through celebration. Deforest affirms the importance of using celebration to help change organizations. "The more today's leaders permit themselves to be creative, conscious celebrators, the more opportunity there is for them to assist in transforming their organizations."[45]

Celebration

When was the last time you ate a meal with the
12 most important people in your life?

When was the last time you dined with your co-workers?

How do you celebrate your personal victories?

Despite our hectic lives, why don't leaders celebrate more often?

What are the core skills of a great celebrator?
Do you know anyone like that?

(Endnotes)

[1] Maslow, A. (1954). *Motivation and Personality.* New York: Van Nostrand.

[2] Heifetz, R.A. (1994). *Leadership Without Easy Answers.* Cambridge, MA: Harvard University Press, p. 126.

[3] Delworth, U, & Hanson, G.R. (1989). *Student Services.* San Francisco: Jossey-Bass.

[4] Coleman, R.E. (1964). *The Master Plan of Evangelism.* Grand Rapids, MI: Baker Book House, p. 33.

[5] Hwang, P.O. (1995). *Other Esteem: A Creative Response to a Society Obsessed with Promoting the Self.* San Diego, CA: Black Forrest Press, p. 116.

[6] Baird, K. (1990). *Creative Leadership.* Fullerton, CA: R.C. Law, p. 79.

[7] Baird, K. (1977). *The Willingness of Polytrophic and Authoritarian Leaders to Utilize a System Approach to Problem Solving.* Doctoral dissertation, United States International University, p. 14.

[8] Ibid., p. 14.

[9] Ibid.

[10] Covey, S.R. (1989). *Principle-Centered Leadership: Teaching People How to Fish.* Provo, UT: Executive Excellence, p. 108.

[11] Maslow, A. (1954). *Motivation and Personality.* New York: Van Nostrand.

[12] Baird, K. (1977). *The Willingness of Polytrophic and Authoritarian Leaders to Utilize a System Approach to Problem Solving.* Doctoral dissertation, United States International University, p. 32.

[13] Ibid., p. 36.

[14] Ibid., p. 51.

[15] Ibid., p. 39.

[16] Owyoung (1978). *A Biblical Evaluation of Secular Leadership Styles in Light of the Ministry of Jesus Christ as Servant Leaders.*

[17] Starratt, R.J. (1993). *The Drama of Leadership.* Washington, D. C.: Falmer Press.

[18] Ibid., p. 118.

[19] Bergquist (1993). *The Postmodern Organization: Mastering the Art of Irreversible Change.* San Francisco: Jossey-Bass.

[20] Starratt, R.J. (1993). *The Drama of Leadership.* Washington, D.C.: Falmer Press, p. 85.

[21] Hughes, R.L., Ginnett, R.C., & Curphy, G.J. (1993). *Leadership: Enhancing the Lessons of Experience.* Boston: Irwin, p. 330.

[22] Renesch, J. (Ed.). (1995). *New Traditions in Business.* San Francisco: Berrett-Koehler, p. 66.

[23] Psalmonds, G. (1958). *A Comparison of the Leadership Techniques of Jesus with the Techniques of Leadership Employed Today.* Doctoral dissertation, Southwestern Baptist Theological Seminary.

[24] Jordan, J.P. (1990). *Secular and Presbyterian Philosophies of Leadership as Compared with the Teaching and Example of Jesus Christ.* Doctoral dissertation, San Francisco Theological Seminary, p. 133.

[25] Senge, P.M. (1990). *The Fifth Discipline.* New York: Double Day, p. 4.

[26] Ibid. p. 4.

[27] Mink, O.G., Mink, B.P., Downes, E.A., & Owen, K.Q. (1994). *Open Organizations: A Model for Effectiveness, Renewal, and Intelligent Change.* San Francisco: Jossey-Bass.

[28] Nair, K. (1994). *A Higher Standard of Leadership.* San Francisco: Jossey-Bass, p. 43.

[29] Ibid., p. 47.

[30] Heifetz, R.A. (1994). *Leadership Without Easy Answers.* Cambridge, MA: Harvard University Press.

[31] Covey, S.R. (1990). *The 7 Habits of Highly Effective People.* New York: Simon & Schuster.

[32] Portnoy, R.A. (1986). *Leadership: What Every Leader Should Know About People.* Englewood Cliffs, NJ: Prentice-Hall, p. 13.

[33] Nair, K. (1994). *A Higher Standard of Leadership.* San Francisco: Jossey-Bass, p. 18.

[34] Starratt, R.J. (1993). *The Drama of Leadership.* Washington, D. C.: Falmer Press, p. 136.

[35] Hwang, P.O. (1995). *Other Esteem: A Creative Response to a Society Obsessed with Promoting the Self.* San Diego, CA: Black Forrest Press, p. 15.

[36] Ibid.

[37] Renesch, J. (Ed.). (1995). *New Traditions in Business.* San Francisco: Berrett-Koehler.

[38] Starratt, R.J. (1993). *The Drama of Leadership.* Washington, D. C.: Falmer Press, p. 120.

[39] Ibid.

[40] Ibid.

[41] Jones, L.B. (1995). *Jesus CEO: Using Ancient Wisdom for Visionary Leadership.* New York: Hyperion, p. 30-31.

[42] DeForest, C. (1986) "The Art of Conscious Celebration: A New Concept for Today's Leaders," in *Transforming Leadership: From Vision to Results.* In Adams, J.D. (Ed.). Alexandria, VA: Miles River Press, 230.

[43] Bryson, J. M., & Crosby, B.C. (1992). *Leadership for the Common Good: Tackling Public Problems in a Shared-Power World.* San Francisco: Jossey-Bass, p. 44-45.

[44] Starratt, R.J. (1993). *The Drama of Leadership.* Washington, D. C.: Falmer Press, p. 5.

[45] DeForest, C. (1986) "The Art of Conscious Celebration: A New Concept for Today's Leaders," in *Transforming Leadership: From Vision to Results.* In Adams, J.D. Alexandria, (Ed.). VA: Miles River Press, 215.

3

Jesus Motivated His Followers

Delayed Gratification

Hope/Faith

Encouragement

Interdependence/Collaboration

Empowerment

Recruitment & Selection

How Jesus Motivated His Followers

*H*followers are not mobilized, any movement will expire. Harnessing the followers' energy and inspiring them to enroll into the cause is a challenging task. Jesus was successful in motivating his entourage not only because he provided them with hope and encouraged and empowered them, but also because he was interdependent with them. Jesus was doubly successful when he used these motivational techniques because he had already established growth-fostering relationships with them, which were in turn enhanced by his extraordinary personal characteristics.

Motivating followers is a critical task in practicing leadership, and we should consider this aspect of Jesus' leadership relationship in depth. The person of Jesus, along with his upstanding characteristics and highly developed relational skills, as previously discussed, laid the foundation to further analyze how he motivated his followers.

Jesus recognized his followers' individual talent and potential and motivated them with delayed gratification, hope, faith, encouragement, interdependence, collaboration, empowerment, and by his individual selection of each of them.[1] Jesus encouraged his followers by telling them: "You are the salt of the earth... [and] the light of the world.... [Let] your light shine before men, that they may see your good deeds and praise your Father in heaven" *(Matthew 5:13-14, 16)*. Throughout adverse circumstances, Jesus emotionally supported his retinue. He accomplished this by "lift[ing] their heads and hearts by substituting understanding for fear, and cheerfulness for a sad countenance. 'Be of good cheer' became one of Christ's more familiar phrases."[2] Jesus acknowledged their tribulation and encouraged them to be cheerful anyway.

Jesus advocated interdependence, which he demonstrated in his life by not subscribing to the "lone ranger" ideology. Jesus delegated responsibilities and gave detailed instructions to his followers.[3] For example, in Matthew 21:1-3, Jesus sent two disciples ahead into the village with specific instructions to return with a donkey on which he would ride into Jerusalem. He often requested actions by his followers that might have appeared unusual, but they did as he asked. Even after his death his desires were acted upon. Bietz also cites the example of the "Great Commission," when Jesus instructed his followers in Matthew 28:19 to "...go and make disciples of all nations, baptizing them in the name of the Father and of the Son and of the Holy Spirit...."[4] To this day, this command continues to be fulfilled.

Jesus could have dictatorially and unilaterally ordered his disciples to obey his will, but instead he was a participative leader and included them in the process.[5] Jesus' purpose was not to "preach all the sermons, do all the miracles, right all the wrongs, or solve all the problems. His purpose was to reproduce the life he had in himself from his Father, to re-create his own leadership in his chosen people."[6] Through these and other actions, Jesus treated people equally. It is significant that he empowered women at a time when women were viewed as male property. Jones observes that

> *In the beginning and at the end of the gospel, God gave primary leadership roles to women. Mary literally conceived and helped deliver the message; wealthy women economically supported Jesus and his staff while they were on their mission; and Mary Magdalene and Martha were the first to recognize the miracle of the resurrection when it happened.*[7]

Jesus recognized the value of women and other oppressed groups as a part of his team and enlisted them into the leadership relationship. Jones comments that "Jesus not only inspired others, he enrolled them. He not only excited people, he got them to sign up. He asked his staff out loud and often 'Will you follow me?'"[8] Empowerment was not simply embodied in the recognition of innate worth, but lived out in action, as demonstrated by Jesus.

Jesus built a relationship with his followers and empowered them by collaborating with them on projects. He involved his disciples

Motivating Followers

personally in his work and taught them through modeling. Stephan and Pace cite three examples of this behavior: Jesus' invitation to Peter to walk on the water with him; involving the disciples in the feeding of the five thousand; and when Jesus asked Peter to go fishing for the coin to pay the tax to Caesar.[9]

Jesus delegated important aspects of his ministry to others because he had courage and personal freedom,[10] and was willing to risk letting his disciples represent him. When Jesus left the earth, his disciples were still not ready to assume their leadership roles since they were still struggling with fear.[11] The disciples "had the satisfaction of 'small wins' in their internships, [however] they had never tested their skills in a setting independent of Jesus. So, for them to lead, he had to leave."[12] Jesus empowered them by giving them the real power of choice.

He also provided his followers with instructions on how to use their authority.[13] Jesus gave his disciples tremendous responsibilities, but also held them accountable. Bietz emphasizes the importance of holding followers accountable and cites the "Parable of the Talents" in Matthew 25:14-30 as an example of Jesus teaching his followers about accountability.[14]

Jesus empowered his retinue by giving them personal strength and authority and by holding them accountable. His collaborative, interdependent, empowering approach motivated his followers to fully engage in the leadership relationship with him. Jesus masterfully used delayed gratification to harness his followers to a larger vision and teach them discipline and promised that the rewards would be given later. He taught that *now* is the time to love others and be a servant to them.

Jesus set a stage that was conducive to learning by providing a cultural climate with an atmosphere of openness and impartiality. The growth-fostering relationships that he developed with his followers enhanced his ability to motivate them. By investing in people and meeting their needs Jesus promoted the critical component of trust. The trust established between Jesus and his retinue was the strong foundation from

87

which he built his followers into highly motivated people through the use of encouragement, interdependence, and empowerment.

McGregor developed the concept of Theory X and Theory Y, which reflect the leader's understanding of human nature and belief of what motivates people.[15] Theory X subscribes to the idea that people respond best to extrinsic motivation, because people tend to be lazy and dislike work. Coercion, control, punishment, and reward are characteristics utilized in the Theory X management of people. Theory Y assumes that people are motivated by intrinsic rewards. This approach holds that people are imaginative and creative, and under the proper conditions they will flourish in their commitment to achieving organizational objectives. This theory is a cooperative theory, which integrates the organization's objectives with the individual's needs.

Theory Z was developed by Ouchi as an alternative approach to Theory X and Theory Y.[16] Theory Z

> ...emphasizes a participation approach to management with a holistic orientation that incorporates the involvement of workers in all facets of the organization. Theory Z is most like the model Jesus devised to instruct his disciples in the formation of early church leadership.[17]

Theory Z leaders invest in their followers' long-term development. Leaders train, educate, and meet the needs of the followers to better equip the followers for effective collaboration. The cultural climate in a Theory Z organization is "innovative [and] abounds because everyone communicates laterally and horizontally in the organizational structure. Ideas are born through interaction, and the vision for the organization proceeds to develop and be defined as people explore ideas and concepts together."[18] Theory Z is based on a servant leadership concept.

Delayed Gratification

The path Jesus laid out for his followers was not full of immediate gratification. It was a path that invested in the future and delayed fulfillment and reward until the end, where Jesus promised future rewards in heaven. In Matthew 5:11-12, Jesus stated, "Blessed are you when people insult you, persecute you and falsely say all kinds of evil against you because of me. Rejoice and be glad, because great is your reward in heaven...."

Another example of delayed reward is found in Luke 6:20-23. Looking at his disciples, Jesus said:

> "Blessed are you who are poor, for yours is the kingdom of God. Blessed are you who hunger now, for you will be satisfied. Blessed are you who weep now, for you will laugh. Blessed are you when men hate you, when they exclude you and insult you and reject your name as evil, because of the Son of Man. Rejoice in that day and leap for joy, because great is your reward in heaven. For that is how their fathers treated the prophets."

Jesus' forward thinking of reward continued in his admonition to invite the lame, crippled, and poor to banquets even though they could not repay the kindness. Jesus assured the hosts that their reward would be in heaven (Luke 14:13-14). The emphasis on delayed gratification provided hope for the future and motivation in the here and now.

Jesus also stressed the importance of waiting for the reward and not showing off one's good works. This point is made in Matthew 6:4 when he told them to give their offerings in secret, so that "your Father, who sees what is done in secret, will reward you." Another example is found in Matthew 6:16-18, where Jesus tells them to make sure that they do not look somber and disfigure their faces when they fast "so it will not be obvious to men that you are fasting, but only to your Father, who is unseen; and

your Father, who sees what is done in secret, will reward you."
Research also shows that children who are able to delay
gratification tend to be more successful than those who are not
able to delay their gratification.[19]

Delayed Gratification

What does it mean to "actively wait?"

What forces in our environment cause us to want
instant gratification?
Why is the desire for immediate gratification dangerous?

Describe a time when you were both patient and persistent.
What was the outcome?

Practice saying "no" to yourself for some small thing that you
want at least one time a day for the next week.
Journal at the end of each day and describe what happened.

Do you believe that doing good is ultimately rewarded?
Why or why not?

It appears that Jesus called his disciples to a life of
insult and persecution. What kind of vision would someone have
to have for you to follow him or her under those conditions?

Hope / Faith

Jesus offered hope to his followers when he told them, "With man this is impossible, but not with God; all things are possible with God" (Mark 10:27). Jesus encouraged his followers by letting them know their significance. He told them, "You are the light of the world. A city on a hill cannot be hidden.... [Let] your light shine before men, that they may see your good deeds and praise your Father in heaven" (Matthew 5:14-16). The devotees of Jesus were reminded of their significance through the use of many analogies (such as the one above) and the following in Matthew 18:12-14, when he said to them:

> "What do you think? If a man owns a hundred sheep, and one of them wanders away, will he not leave the ninety-nine on the hills and go to look for the one that wandered off? And if he finds it, I tell you the truth, he is happier about that one sheep than about the ninety-nine that did not wander off. In the same way your Father in heaven is not willing that any of these little ones should be lost."

Jesus used the parable of the one lost sheep to convey the importance or value of each follower. "I tell you that in the same way there will be more rejoicing in heaven over one sinner who repents than over ninety-nine righteous persons who do not need to repent" (Luke 15:7). In Luke 12:6-7, Jesus noted, "Are not five sparrows sold for two pennies? Yet not one of them is forgotten by God. Indeed, the very hairs of your head are all numbered. Don't be afraid; you are worth more than many sparrows." Jesus let the people know that God knew every detail about them.

Just as forgiveness requires embracing a higher standard, having faith also makes this leap. It is impossible to adequately discuss Jesus' leadership without addressing the topic of faith, which was a powerful resource for him. Through faith he healed people, he saved people, he encouraged people, and provided them with hope. When there appeared to be no hope, Jesus told people just to believe. For example,

> While Jesus was still speaking, some men came from the house of Jairus, the synagogue ruler. "Your daughter is dead," they said. "Why bother the teacher any more?" Ignoring what they said, Jesus told the synagogue ruler, "Don't be afraid; just believe." (Mark 5:35-36)

There are many examples of faith being the instrument used to heal people:

- "Go, said Jesus, "your faith has healed you." Immediately he received his sight and followed Jesus along the road. (Mark 10:52)

- "Daughter, your faith has healed you. Go in peace." (Luke 8:48)

- "Receive your sight; your faith has healed you." (Luke 18:42)

- Some men brought to him a paralytic, lying on a mat. When Jesus saw their faith, he said to the paralytic, "Take heart, son; your sins are forgiven." (Matthew 9:2)

As demonstrated, Jesus praises those with faith. Upon hearing about the powerful Roman centurion who asked Jesus to heal his servant from afar, Jesus "was amazed at him, and turning to the crowd following him, he said, 'I tell you, I have not found such great faith even in Israel'" (Luke 7:9). Jesus also acknowledged the tremendous faith of the widow who put her two small coins in the treasury. Jesus said, "I tell you the truth, this poor widow has put more into the treasury than all the others" (Mark 12:43). It was the condition of the heart that mattered to Jesus, and this woman's faith touched him.

Motivating Followers

Jesus also asserted that lack of faith hindered people. In Matthew 13:54-58, it is explained that after Jesus had come into his hometown of Nazareth the people were offended by his teaching; therefore, "he did not do many miracles there because of their lack of faith." In Luke 8:24-25, there is a story about the disciples' lack of faith.

> The disciples went and woke him, saying, "Master, Master, we're going to drown!" He got up and rebuked the wind and the raging waters; the storm subsided, and all was calm. "Where is your faith?" he asked his disciples. In fear and amazement they asked one another, "Who is this? He commands even the winds and the water, and they obey him."

Jesus taught his followers about the amazing power of faith. Jesus posited, "...whatever you ask for in prayer, believe that you have received it, and it will be yours" (Mark 11:24). When the apostles asked Jesus to increase their faith, he replied, "If you have faith as small as a mustard seed, you can say to this mulberry tree, 'Be uprooted and planted in the sea,' and it will obey you" (Luke 17:6). Jesus emphasized the great power of faith and the importance of having faith when one makes a request.

Jesus did not waste valuable time or energy worrying about things. He posed this rhetorical question: "Who of you by worrying can add a single hour to his life? Since you cannot do this very little thing, why do you worry about the rest?" (Luke 12:25-26). Jesus spent much time adequately instructing and preparing the apostles for their service, but he ultimately left it up to each of them to have faith that everything would work out. He told them, "When you are brought before synagogues, rulers and authorities, do not worry about how you will defend yourselves or what you will say, for the Holy Spirit will teach you at that time what you should say" (Luke 12:11-12).

Jesus provided his followers with the opportunity to choose faith over worry, fear, and doubt. This was a liberating alternative that freed them from a great loss of time and energy. In Matthew 6:25, Jesus' famous words of encouragement are found: "Therefore I tell you, do not worry about your life, what you will eat or drink; or about your body, what you will wear. Is not life more important than food, and the body more important than clothes?" Finally, Jesus encouraged, "Therefore do not worry about tomorrow, for tomorrow will worry about itself. Each day has enough trouble of its own" (Matthew 6:34). Preventing energy loss by not worrying is truly a pearl of wisdom that Jesus presented. Encouraging his followers to have faith was a critical component of Jesus' leadership, and he never ceased challenging them to take the less-traveled road of higher standards.

Bennis included faith, hope, and optimism as components in his list of the ten personal and organizational characteristics that are required to create a learning organization and for coping with change.[20] Scale six on the *Leader Behavior Questionnaire* is based on the assumption that "effective visionary leaders have a basic sense of self-assurance, an underlying belief that they can personally make a difference and have an impact on people, events, and organizational achievements."[21] Covey, in his book *Principle-Centered Leadership*, also emphasizes the importance of having faith, and believing and trusting others. He opines that people reach their full potential when they are treated accordingly.[22]

Motivating Followers

Hope/Faith

What is hope? How can you give another person hope?

What can you do if you're not a hopeful person?

What would a hopeful organization look, sound, and feel like?

What do most employees hope for?
If you don't know, how could you find out?

What is faith to you?
How can faith be expressed in practical terms?
Is anything preventing you from being a trusting person?

Why do some people always seem to be defeated?
Why do others triumph?

Can you find success in surrender? How?

What is the relationship between vision and faith?

Encouragement

$\mathcal{J}$esus encouraged people to have hope (*Mark 5:36*) and also
affirmed their special contributions (*Matthew 26:10*). In a discussion
of Alfred Adler's theories, Corey deduced that "Encouragement
is the most powerful method available for changing a person's
beliefs. It helps [people] build self-confidence and stimulates
courage."[23] Jesus understood the power of encouragement and
gave it liberally to his followers. In a sermon on a mountainside
Jesus encouraged his followers with a comprehensive list of the
"Blessed art thou's," beginning with the poor in spirit and ending
with the persecuted (*Matthew 5:3-11*).

Jesus encouraged his team by letting them know how significant
they were (*Matthew 5:14-16*). Blumenthal stresses the importance
of encouraging people to speak and function as a team in order
to motivate them.[24] He instructed them to shake the dust off
their feet when they leave a town or home that does not welcome
them or listen to their words (*Matthew 10:14*). In Matthew 10:23,
Jesus prepares his disciples for discouragement with these
instructions: "When you are persecuted in one place, flee to
another. I tell you the truth, you will not finish going through the
cities of Israel before the Son of Man comes." Jesus' anticipation
of discouragement and preparation of how to deal with it served
to encourage his disciples.

At times Jesus directly encouraged specific people. When Jairus
thought his daughter was dead, Jesus told him, "Don't be afraid;
just believe" (*Mark 5:36*). In another example, Jesus told the mother
of a demon-possessed girl in Matthew 15:28, "'Woman, you have
great faith! Your request is granted.' And her daughter was
healed from that very hour." And, Jesus encouraged the woman
who poured expensive perfume on him by defending her in the
midst of her critics and telling them that she had done a beautiful
thing to him (*Matthew 26:10*). Even in Jesus' last moment of life he
encouraged the thief on the cross next to him with the words, "I
tell you the truth, today you will be with me in paradise"
(*Luke 23:43*). As we have seen, Jesus encouraged people through

Motivating Followers

rewarding their faith, granting their requests, and public affirmation.

Jesus not only affirmed others; he received affirmation himself. At his baptism "a voice came from heaven: 'You are my Son, whom I love; with you I am well pleased'" (Mark 1:11). Jesus was affirmed again at the transfiguration in the presence of James, John, and Peter: "A voice came from the cloud, saying, 'This is my Son, whom I have chosen; listen to him'" (Luke 9:35). Matthew writes that Jesus was here

> ...to fulfill what was spoken through the prophet Isaiah: "Here is my servant whom I have chosen, the one I love, in whom I delight; I will put my Spirit on him, and he will proclaim justice to the nations.... In his name the nations will put their hope." (Matthew 12:17-18, 21)

Jesus received encouragement from his father in heaven and in turn encouraged others by affirming them and providing hope for the future.

After his resurrection, Jesus continued to encourage his disciples through his presence when he stood among them and told them, "Peace be with you" (Luke 24:36). He called them to build a firm foundation and achieve praxis as

> "...everyone who hears these words of mine and puts them into practice is like a wise man who built his house on the rock. The rain came down, the streams rose, and the winds blew and beat against that house; yet it did not fall, because it had its foundation on the rock." (Matthew 7:24-25)

This firm foundation of hope and encouragement helped motivate his followers to press on toward their goals.

Encouragement

Why would leaders want to plan and prepare
people for discouragement?

What does it mean to be accountable for your talent?

Why is delegated authority for leaders
and those around them encouraging?

What are some other ways for leaders to encourage
the people around them?

Describe a time when you tried to encourage someone
by focusing on their weaknesses. What happened?

Which do you analyze more, your successes or your failures?

Describe a situation when you could have acted unethically
or immorally and chose not to.

How can leaders learn to view every challenge
and setback as encouraging?

Interdependence/Collaboration

Because of his tremendous competence, Jesus could have been a "lone ranger" in his crusade; however, he had a bigger plan, which included group participation. In Matthew 16:16-17, Peter said to Jesus, "You are the Christ, the Son of the living God." Jesus then blessed Peter and told him that these words were the "rock" upon which

> *"...I will build my church, and the gates of Hades will not overcome it. I will give you the keys of the kingdom of heaven; whatever you bind on earth will be bound in heaven, and whatever you loose on earth will be loosed in heaven."*
> (Matthew 16:18-19)

Jesus' approach was interdependent as he declared that Peter's profession of faith was a foundation for the process of building his church.

Jesus included the disciples in his miracles, such as the feeding of five thousand people with only five loaves of bread and two fishes. In Luke 9:16-17, "he gave thanks...and gave [the loaves and fishes] to the disciples to set before the people. They all ate and were satisfied, and the disciples picked up twelve basketfuls of broken pieces that were left over." Jesus' participative approach gave the disciples a sense of contribution in the process of leadership. The disciples experienced Jesus' need for their help as he created a collaborative environment that produced a much larger movement than it would have been had he not included others.

Today, collaboration helps solve some of the problems that our communities face. "The crisis is that we as a people don't know how to come together to solve these problems. We lack the capacities to address the issues or remove the obstacles that stand in the way of public deliberation."[25] Lappe & Du Bois continue to say that it is only "when more and more citizens perceive themselves as having a stake in solving our problems and believe in themselves as problem solvers" that we will make headway in solving our mounting problems.[26] This concept of stakeholder involvement is rapidly growing, leaving its mark on everything from marketing to evaluations.

Another time Jesus showed interdependence was when he delegated to Peter the responsibility of paying the annual two-drachma per person temple tax for them. (A drachma was a silver coin worth about a day's wage.) Jesus told Peter to go fishing and "Take the first fish you catch; open its mouth and you will find a four-drachma coin. Take it and give it to them for my tax and yours" (Matthew 17:24-27). Jesus took the time to explain to Peter the importance of paying the tax so that others would not be offended and that as the Son of God he should be exempt from paying it; however, it was more important to be courteous.

Jesus was not only interdependent with his own team, but chose to work with, not against, people on the same side of the cause. In Luke 9:49-50, John said to Jesus, "Master...we saw a man driving out demons in your name and we tried to stop him, because he is not one of us." "Do not stop him," Jesus said, "for whoever is not against you is for you." Again in Luke 11:17, Jesus emphasized unity and proclaimed to them "Any kingdom divided against itself will be ruined, and a house divided against itself will fall." Jesus fully included his followers into the leadership process and made it clear that "the kingdom of God is within you" (Luke 17:21).

Jesus knew that his team would be more effective if his followers were unified and did not compare themselves to others or feel resentment and jealousy. He emphasized this point in the story of the prodigal son when he spoke of the faithful son's refusal to join in the celebration for his disobedient brother's safe return, and the father's response:

> "My son," the father said, "you are always with
> me, and everything I have is yours. But we had to
> celebrate and be glad, because this brother of yours

Motivating Followers

was dead and is alive again; he was lost and is found." (Luke 15:31-32)

Jesus capitalized on the beauty of forgiveness and reconciliation and used this parable to teach about the power of unity.

Jesus was inclusive and utilized people's gifts in the best way possible. For example, when Jesus was getting in the boat to leave Decapolis, the man whom he had delivered from demon possession wanted to go with him. However, Jesus knew that this man would be more effective carrying the cause to his hometown, so he told him to stay in Decapolis. The man then began to tell how much Jesus had done for him, and all the people were amazed (Mark 5:18-20).

Jesus' leadership model might best be described as interdependent, and his followers fully participated in the leadership process with him. He said in Luke 17:21 that the "kingdom of God is within you." This is a profound proclamation of interdependence and Jesus acknowledged, "You are those who have stood by me in my trials" (Luke 22:28). Clearly, this was participative leadership.

Hwang explains that, "interdependency within an organization...is the acknowledgment and practice of believing in the vital contribution of each employee within the organization. It is the mutual respect for one another and the support of everyone's role and function."[27] It is evident that Jesus believed in the essential contribution of each member of his team. Jesus could have done many tasks on his own without the assistance of others, but chose to humbly include them in the process. Hwang deduces that "interdependency is...an exercise in humility."[28]

Gordon, who advocates paying attention to the wisdom of the group, finds that his "experience as a consultant...convinces [him] that most leaders greatly underestimate the wealth of knowledge, ideas, and ingenuity lying untapped in the heads of group members."[29] Jesus' band of followers was not made up of the most extraordinary group of people available, but Jesus could

101

Interdependence/Collaboration

see the assets that each one brought to the leadership process and developed each one individually.

When employers genuinely make "workers feel it's their company, they develop an enhanced sense of responsibility for what happens in their organization."[30] Jesus fully included his followers into the leadership process. An example of Jesus helping to make his followers feel that it was their organization occurred when Jesus told Peter, "I will give you the keys of the kingdom of heaven..." *(Matthew 16:19)*. Companies are learning that "the closer the workers feel to the company, the more their frontline experience informs the core decision-making that creates business success."[31] This climate provides an excellent opportunity for employers and employees to practice leadership *Courteous Rebel*-style.

Motivating Followers

Interdependence/Collaboration

Why are some leaders afraid to depend on others?

Describe a time when you were facing a great challenge and trusted another person enough to allow them to support you. What was the result?

Explain the meaning of this saying:
"Whoever is not against you is for you." Do you believe this? What are the actions of a person who believes this?

When was the last time you asked for help?

Do you know the unique gifts of each person in your workplace? If not, how could you discover their gifts?

Why do you think Jesus had disciples and didn't just do everything himself?

How do you think Jesus chose his disciples? How do you?

Would Jesus choose you today? Why or why not?

What's the worst that could happen if people don't work together? What's the best?

Do you think most people feel like they make a difference? How could you make every person who comes in contact with you know that they make a difference?

Empowerment

*J*esus knew the value of empowerment in motivating his followers. He empowered them, and in return they made a deeper commitment to the leadership relationship. With power came responsibility, which led to great commitment from his followers. In Luke 9:1-2, when Jesus had called "the Twelve together, he gave them power and authority to drive out all demons and to cure diseases, and he sent them out to preach the kingdom of God and to heal the sick." In Luke 22:29, he empowered them by telling them, "And I confer on you a kingdom, just as my Father conferred one on me...." Jesus did not just give lip service to empowerment; he gave them real power.

After the resurrection, the eleven remaining apostles went to a mountain in Galilee where Jesus conferred upon them the Great Commission.

> *"All authority in heaven and on earth has been given to me. Therefore go and make disciples of all nations, baptizing them in the name of the Father and of the Son and of the Holy Spirit, and teaching them to obey everything I have commanded you. And surely I am with you always, to the very end of the age."*
> *(Matthew 28:18-20)*

Jesus provided encouragement and reassurance when he harnessed his followers to a great challenge and empowered them to act.

With real power comes much responsibility. Jesus asserted, "From everyone who has been given much, much will be demanded and from the one who has been entrusted with much, much more will be asked" *(Luke 12:48b)*. Luke 16:10-12 exemplifies Jesus' great requirement of being faithful in the little things:

"Whoever can be trusted with very little can also be trusted with much, and whoever is dishonest with very little will also be dishonest with much. So if you have not been trustworthy in handling worldly wealth, who will trust you with true riches? And if you have not been trustworthy with someone else's property, who will give you property of your own?"

In this passage, Jesus emphasized the care that must be taken when delegating power to others. Clearly, their competence in handling responsibility must be taken into account.

Jesus told parables to his followers that highlighted his point about responsibility. The "Parable of the Talents" deals with monetary investments. [Note: a talent was worth more than a thousand dollars.] A man was going on a journey and entrusted his assets to his servants according to their ability. To one he gave five talents, another two talents, and to the last, one talent. The two servants who were given five and two talents had doubled their profits by the time the man came home.

"But the man who had received the one talent went off, dug a hole in the ground and hid his master's money. After a long time the master of those servants returned and settled accounts with them." (Matthew 25:18-19)

The two men who increased their talents were praised by their master and he put them in charge of many more things. However, he ordered that the talent be taken from the man who did not multiply it, and that the talent be given to the one who now had the ten talents *(Matthew 25:14-28)*.

In Luke 10:19, Jesus affirmed that he had "given [the disciples] authority to... overcome all the power of the enemy...." Having given them this tremendous power, Jesus required significant commitment and accountability from his followers, yet also provided the support for them to succeed as they were empowered. He reminded them, "And anyone who does not carry his cross and follow me cannot be my disciple" (Luke 14:27).

Leadership should be educative and empowering, according to Foster.[32] By educating collaborators throughout the process, they are more likely to vacillate in and out of the leader's role and be empowered to start another leadership project in which they become leaders. Teaching people how to make a difference, and inspiring them to persevere throughout the process, serves as a springboard for effecting much change in many different arenas.

Tannenbaum[33] confirms that empowering others does not necessarily translate into losing power for oneself. The idea of expanding power is when a leader empowers another to use power; it is creating more power, not just draining a resource of a finite amount of power. This is not to say that to empower sometimes does not mean giving away the responsibility that is attendant with that power. If the power is relinquished wisely, then power is expanded and greater things can happen. Moreover, empowerment increases the leader's range of managing more power and ultimately creates something more extraordinary than what could have been done without empowerment.

Jesus' followers were collaborators who were fully engaged in the process of leadership with him. His stance was congruent with Burns' idea that

> The arena of power is no longer the exclusive preserve of a power elite or an establishment or persons clothed with legitimacy. Power is ubiquitous; it permeates human relationships. It exists whether or not it is quested for. It is the glory and the burden of most of humanity.[34]

Jesus understood this burden of power and testified to his followers that with more power comes more responsibility (Luke 12:48b). Empowerment not only puts greater responsibility

Motivating Followers

on the empowered, but it also causes leaders to be held more accountable, thus encouraging higher ethical and moral standards.

Jesus also included his disciples in his miracles. For example, he delegated to his disciples the responsibility of passing out the bread and fish (that he had multiplied to the multitudes of people.) Another time, he gave Peter the responsibility to go and pay the four-drachma temple tax for them with a coin that he found in a fish's mouth. Covey asserts that, "Delegation makes the difference between the independent producer and the interdependent manager or leader. Properly done, delegation enables one to accomplish much more work in the same amount of time by multiplying one's strength through others...."[35]

Apparently, Jesus knew that empowering his followers would facilitate them to make a deeper commitment to this leadership relationship. House[36] found that empowerment also heightened followers' expectations of themselves. The collaborators' enlightenment of their newfound power influences the relationship greatly. Collaborators can be more engaged because they believe they can make a difference and know they have a higher stake in the process. The collaborators' greater exercise of power can also help keep the leaders and organization in check with ethical guidelines.

Empowerment

*Why are many leaders reluctant to include their followers
in decision-making?*

*What concerns you about sharing your power
and authority with someone else?*

*Are you willing to give power to another person?
Would you feel ultimately responsible for the results for having
entrusted someone with that power?*

*Describe a time when you were faithful and diligent
with a small task and were later rewarded with even more
responsibility and authority. How did that feel?*

Do you have any talents that you're hiding? Why?

*What does dynamic power look like?
What would you do if you had dynamic power?*

Motivating Followers

Individual Recruitment & Selection

Another way Jesus empowered his disciples was by individually selecting them. He did not take out ads or just take in anyone who wanted to join his inner circle. The following verses demonstrate the way that Jesus individually called his disciples:

> • *Going on from there, he saw two other brothers, James son of Zebedee and his brother John. They were in a boat with their father Zebedee, preparing their nets. Jesus called them, and immediately they left the boat and their father and followed him.* (Matthew 4: 21-22)

> • *"Come, follow me," Jesus said, "and I will make you fishers of men." At once they left their nets and followed him.* (Mark 1:17-18)

> • *As he walked along, he saw Levi son of Alphaeus sitting at the tax collector's booth. "Follow me," Jesus told him, and Levi got up and followed him.* (Mark 2:14)

After Jesus initially selected his disciples, he formally appointed them in public. It is noted in Mark 3:13-14, that "Jesus went up on a mountainside and called to him those he wanted, and they came to him. He appointed twelve—designating them apostles—that they might be with him and that he might send them out to preach...." after the disciples received training, Jesus called the twelve to him, and "he sent them out two by two and gave them authority over evil spirits" (Mark 6:7b). Jesus commissioned them to "Go into all the world and preach the good news to all creation" (Mark 16:15). No doubt the empowerment of the disciples' public affirmation of their appointment helped to motivated them.

Jesus had tremendous expectations for his disciples since he had specifically called them to make a commitment to this cause. As a reward for this commitment Jesus reassured his followers that "everyone who has left houses or brothers or sisters or father or mother or children or fields for my sake will receive a hundred times as much and will inherit eternal life. But many who are first will be last, and many who are last will be first" (Matthew 19:29-30). Yes, the commitment Jesus required was colossal; but he equipped his followers to succeed by developing interdependent relationships, and through empowering and encouraging them.

Jesus individually invited his disciples to be a part of his leadership team (Matthew 4:18-22 & 9:9). Cumming affirms the importance of the invitation to the participants when he says, "The planning phase—especially the selection and invitation of stakeholders—is a crucial task."[37] Jesus was able to elicit a deep commitment from his disciples because he was able to enroll them into the mission.

In the industrial paradigm, the concept of getting others on one's side was expressed as "buying in." Senge and others subscribe to a new way of thinking, which "enrolls" people into a commitment. Buying implies selling, whereas enrolling implies free choice and commitment.[38]

> The committed person brings an energy, passion, and excitement that cannot be generated if you are only compliant, even genuinely compliant.... A group of people truly committed to a common vision is an awesome force. They can accomplish the seemingly impossible.[39]

Motivating Followers

Individual Recruitment & Selection

Have you ever been uniquely chosen for something?
How did you feel?

How is an individual invitation different than
the idea of "buying in"? Why should leaders care?

Why did the disciples follow Jesus?

Can strong and talented people ever be followers?

What's the difference between compliance and obedience?

What kind of training did you receive to advance
your life and career?

What kind of training do you wish you had received?

(Endnotes)

[1] Stephan, E., & Pace, W. (1990). *The Perfect Leader: Following Christ's Example to Leadership Success.* Salt Lake City: Deseret Book.

[2] Ibid., p. 27.

[3] Bietz, R.R. (1980). *Jesus the Leader.* Nampa, ID: Pacific Press.

[4] Ibid.

[5] Jordan, J.P. (1990). *Secular and Presbyterian Philosophies of Leadership as Compared with the Teaching and Example of Jesus Christ.* Doctoral dissertation, San Francisco Theological Seminary.

[6] Ford, L. (1991). *Transforming Leadership: Jesus' Way of Creating Vision, Shaping Values, and Empowering Change.* Downers Grove, IL: InterVarsity, p. 200.

[7] Jones, L.B. (1995). *Jesus CEO: Using Ancient Wisdom for Visionary Leadership.* New York: Hyperion, p. 191.

[8] Ibid., p. 240.

[9] Stephan, E., & Pace, W. (1990). *The Perfect Leader: Following Christ's Example to Leadership Success.* Salt Lake City: Deseret Book.

[10] Jordan, J.P. (1990). *Secular and Presbyterian Philosophies of Leadership as Compared with the Teaching and Example of Jesus Christ.* Doctoral dissertation, San Francisco Theological Seminary.

[11] McKenna, D.L. (1989). *Power to Follow Grace to Lead.* Dallas: Word Publishing.

[12] Ibid., p. 176.

[13] Jones, L.B. (1995). *Jesus CEO: Using Ancient Wisdom for Visionary Leadership.* New York: Hyperion, p. 263.

[14] Bietz, R.R. (1980). *Jesus the Leader.* Nampa, ID: Pacific Press.

[15] McGregor in Drushal (1987). *Attitudes Toward Participative Decision-Making Among Church Leaders: A Comparison of the Influences of Nominal Group Technique, Delphi Survey Technique, and Social Judgment Analysis.* Drushal, Mary E.; Dissertation Abstracts International, Vol 47 (8-A), Feb 1987, p. 48.

[16] Ouchi (1981) in Drushal (1987). *Attitudes Toward Participative Decision-Making Among Church Leaders: A Comparison of the Influences of Nominal Group Technique, Delphi Survey Technique, and Social Judgment Analysis.* Drushal, Mary E.; Dissertation Abstracts International, Vol 47(8-A), Feb 1987.

[17] Drushal (1987). *Attitudes Toward Participative Decision-Making Among Church Leaders: A Comparison of the Influences of Nominal Group Technique, Delphi Survey Technique, and Social Judgment Analysis.* Drushal, Mary E.; Dissertation Abstracts International, Vol 47(8-A), Feb 1987, p. 48.

[18] Ibid., p. 52.

[19] Goleman, D. (1997). *Emotional Intelligence.* New York: Bantam Books.

[20] Bennis, W. (1989). *On Becoming a Leader.* New York: Addison-Wesley Publishing.

112

Motivating Followers

[21] Sashkin, M., & Burke, W.W. (1990). *Understanding and Assessing Organizational Leadership.* In K. Clark & M. Clark (Eds.), *Measures of Leadership.* West Orange, NJ: Leadership Library of America, p. 312.

[22] Covey, S.R. (1989). *Principle-Centered Leadership: Teaching People How to Fish.* Provo, UT: Executive Excellence.

[23] Corey, G. (1991). *Theory and Practice of Counseling and Psychotherapy.* Pacific Grove, CA: Brooks/Cole, p. 142.

[24] Tichy, N.M., & Devanna, M.A. (1986). *The Transformational Leader.* New York: John Wiley & Sons, p. 241.

[25] Lappe, F.M., & Du Bois, P.M. (1994). *The Quickening of America.* San Francisco: Jossey-Bass, p. 9.

[26] Ibid., p. 17.

[27] Hwang, P.O. (1995). *Other Esteem: A Creative Response to a Society Obsessed with Promoting the Self.* San Diego, CA: Black Forrest Press, p. 115.

[28] Ibid., p. 115.

[29] Gordon, T. (1977). *Leader Effectiveness Training.* USA: Wyden Books, p. 38.

[30] Lappe, F.M., & Du Bois, P.M. (1994). *The Quickening of America.* San Francisco: Jossey-Bass, p. 90.

[31] Ibid., p. 82.

[32] Foster, W. (1989). *Toward a Critical Practice of Leadership.* In J. Smyth (Ed.), *Critical Perspectives on Educational Leadership* (pp. 39-62). Philadelphia: Falmer Press.

[33] Tannenbaum, R. (1968). *Control in Organizations.* New York: McCrawHill.

[34] Burns, J.M. (1977). *Leadership.* New York: Harper & Row, p. 15.

[35] Covey, S.R. (1989). *Principle-Centered Leadership: Teaching People How to Fish.* Provo, UT: Executive Excellence, p. 107.

[36] House, R.J. (1984). *Power in Organizations: A Social Psychological Perspective.* Unpublished manuscript, University of Toronto, Canada.

[37] Weisbord, M.R. (1992). *Discovering Common Ground: How Future Search Conferences bring People Together to Achieve Breakthrough Innovation, Empowerment, Shared Vision, and Collaborative Action.* San Francisco: Berrett-Koehler, p. 376.

[38] Senge, P.M. (1990). *The Fifth Discipline.* New York: Double Day.

[39] Ibid., p. 221.

4

Key Leadership Functions:

Power

Conflict

Transformational leadership

Servant Leadership

Leadership through Example

Sacrifice

Purpose

Vision

Planning

Priorities

A Higher Standard

Forgiveness

Key Leadership Functions

The foundation of our analysis has been laid through the discourse on Jesus' characteristics, the relationships that he developed with his followers, and the exploration of how he motivated people. To conclude this analysis on Jesus' leadership, it is necessary to address some of the core issues related to leadership such as power, conflict, transformational leadership, servant leadership, leadership by example, sacrifice, purpose, vision, planning, priorities, higher standards, and forgiveness.

A servant leader needs humility complemented by congruence in thought and action; but without purpose, vision, and planning his leadership will not effect change. Fortunately, Jesus had a vision that was bolstered by specific purposes. Leaders have no shortage of followers when they offer a higher purpose to them.[1] Proverbs 29:18 supports the need for vision: "Where there is no vision, the people will perish." Jesus envisioned the larger picture and pursued that image, even when the details were unknown to him.[2]

McKenna divided Jesus' visioning into four categories[3]— meaningful vision, motivating vision, mobilizing vision, and focused vision. The first type is *meaningful* vision, which focuses on the primary purpose of vision. Jesus is clear about the meaning of his mission in John 10:9-10:

> I am the gate; whoever enters through me will be saved. He will come in and go out, and find pasture. The thief comes only to steal and kill and destroy; I have come that they may have life, and have it to the full.

The second type is *motivating* vision, which establishes the foundation for following the vision. Jesus' motivating vision was to seek the lost. His was not a self-enthroning or self-aggrandizing dream, because everything Jesus focused on was for the good of humankind.

The third type is *mobilizing* vision. McKenna reports, "Unless the vision of a leader mobilizes the energies of persons and the resources of an organization, it will fail."[4] Jesus was very successful at this step of the process. The results of his initial mobilization have been like a small pebble dropped into the proverbial pond—the ripples extend indefinitely.

The fourth type is *focused* vision. While Jesus initial vision had purpose and motivation—to offer spiritual life to the world—the details of the implementation were developed during the course of his three-year ministry. As Jesus' career advanced, his vision became clearer and more specific.[5] At times it was specifically painful—so much so that in the Garden of Gethsemane he asked that this "cup," or burden, be lifted from him.

Besides possessing a clear vision, Jesus had a plan and he gave his staff clear instructions on how to implement it.[6] Jesus

> ...*was able to create, articulate, and communicate a compelling vision; to change what people talk about and dream of; to make his followers transcend self-interest; to enable us to see ourselves and our world in a new way; to provide prophetic insight into the very heart of things; and to bring about the highest order of change.*[7]

Regarding the visionary aspect of Jesus' leadership, Ford[8] has synthesized seven points that describe how Jesus accomplished this feat. These points claim that Jesus was a seer who lived by the unseen (faith). His visions were practical and "down-to-earth," of the largest and widest scope, personal, realistic, radical, and hopeful.[9] In addition to these defining aspects of Jesus' vision to "seek and save the lost," McKenna operationalizes that vision.[10] The author offers the following components of operations for motivating followers, mobilizing resources, and monitoring performance:[11]

Authority:	*The name of Jesus*
Timing:	*Urgency*
Task:	*Make disciples*
Geography:	*All nations*
Symbol:	*Baptism*
Skill:	*Teaching*
Subject:	*The word of Christ*
Outcome:	*Obedience to commands of Christ*
Promise:	*Christ's presence*
Term:	*To the very end of the age*

(Matthew 28:16-20)

While pursuing his vision, Jesus continuously faced conflict. The types of conflict that Jesus encountered in the Gospel of Mark, as categorized by McKenna included public conflict (e.g., when disciples failed to heal the epileptic boy); interpersonal (e.g., when disciples argued over who would be the greatest in the kingdom); and intergroup (e.g., conflict over who has the authority to minister).[12] The manner in which Jesus handled these conflicts set him far above the average guru. Ford analyzes the way Jesus dealt with conflict and the reasons that he had the ability to do each of the following:[13]

1. *Discern motives: "Jesus knew their hypocrisy"* (Mark 12:16).

2. *Sense ill will and danger: "Why are you trying to trap me?" he asked* (Mark 12:16).

3. *Deflect attacks: His usual approach was to answer a question with a question—"Who do you say that I am?"* (Matthew 15:15).

4. *See the heart of a matter: He discerned the basic point at issue—"And the rich young ruler went away with a heavy heart"* (Mark 10:22).

5. *Challenge the questioners' consciences*

6. *Know when to stop: He stated the principle, but let the Pharisees draw out the implications and apply it* (Mark 12:13-17). *Jesus' consistent response to this kind of criticism was to force the question, detect prejudice,*

> *expose the issue in depth and at its heart,*
> *and then return it as a challenge to the*
> *questioner. Also, Mark notes that Jesus'*
> *opponents were amazed at him and from then*
> *on did not dare ask him any more questions*
> *(Mark 12:34).*

Jesus was a master at dealing with conflict. In each situation that involved conflict he manifested patience.[14] He did not enter into an argument over the apparent problem, but rather, he

> *...began with a diagnosis of the root cause and*
> *proceeded to resolve the conflict by bringing the*
> *disciples to common ground and then lifting their*
> *sights to a higher, common cause. For the*
> *interpersonal conflict over who would be the*
> *greatest in the kingdom of heaven, Jesus did not*
> *rebuke their ambition. Instead he linked greatness*
> *with servanthood, thus reinforcing his mission once*
> *again in the minds of the apostles.[15]*

Jesus wisely manipulated the baser elements in the disciples' personalities by transforming their vision to a higher plane. Everyone was called to a more elevated ground when he emphasized the *spirit* of the law and de-emphasized the *letter* of the law.[16]

Many conflicts that Jesus faced were centered around breaking customs. In John 5:1-14, Jesus healed a disabled man on the Sabbath who was laying by the pool at Bethesda. This man had been an invalid for 38 years, and Youssef[17] cites the example of Jesus putting human needs before religious customs. Jesus directed people to the spirit of the law and at the same time confronted the religious leaders about having elevated the commandments into gods.[18]

By shifting the emphasis away from legalism, Jesus did not fit the mold in which others tried to put him. He broke away from the restrictive traditions of the elders, which encouraged his followers to do likewise.[19] Jesus took a revolutionary stance against the status quo and was "willing to go against the teachings and religious understandings of those people of the highest cultural level in his society."[20] In the face of conflict, Jesus always retained the higher moral ground.

Power

*I*t is appropriate to begin the section of key leadership functions with the issue of power, since many of the other functions are influenced by it. Jesus radiated power. Luke 6:19 reports that "the people all tried to touch him, because power was coming from him and healing them all." In Mark 13:26 it is noted that eventually "men will see the Son of Man coming in clouds with great power and glory."

Jesus had great power at his disposal, but at times he chose not to use it. In Matthew 26:53, when he was being arrested by a detachment of 300-600 Roman soldiers and the Jewish officials, Jesus asserted, "Do you think I cannot call on my Father, and he will at once put at my disposal more than twelve legions of angels?" (Note: a "legion"—which was the largest unit of the Roman army—consisted of 3,000-6,000 highly trained, disciplined, and fearsome soldiers.) Jesus used "12 legions" to signify an incredibly large number of soldiers that those present at his arrest could relate to, and to impart a vivid image of the power available to him. Jesus was not afraid to embrace his power; he just chose to use it for others' best interests. He used his power to heal people (*Mark 5:29*), to cast out demons (*Mark 1:25-26*), and to teach people (*Matthew 5-7*). In fact, he had so much power that he didn't need to use his power "over" people. Instead he used power to empower others.

Jesus knew where his power resources were. When his disciples could not drive out a demon, they asked "Why?" (*Mark 9:28*). Jesus then taught them about the great resource of power they had in prayer (*Mark 9:29*). Not only was Jesus aware *of* his power resources, he was able to perceive when any power had proceeded *from* him. When a woman who had been bleeding from an internal hemorrhage for 12 years came up behind Jesus in a crowd and touched the fringe of his cloak, "Immediately her bleeding stopped and she felt in her body that she was freed from her suffering. At once Jesus realized that power had gone out from him. He turned around in the crowd and asked, 'Who touched my clothes?'" *(Mark 5:29-30).*

Being completely humble and confident simultaneously, Jesus was able to maintain his humility while at the same time possessing colossal power. He encouraged his followers to humble themselves as he did. To emphasize this point, Luke recounts a story about a man of great power who humbled himself before Jesus by sending some Jewish elders to him asking that he come to his house and save the life of his beloved servant.

> *So Jesus went with them. He was not far from the house when the centurion sent friends to say to him: "Lord, don't trouble yourself, for I do not deserve to have you come under my roof. That is why I did not even consider myself worthy to come to you. But say the word, and my servant will be healed. For I myself am a man under authority, with soldiers under me. I tell this one, 'Go,' and he goes; and that one, 'Come,' and he comes. I say to my servant, 'Do this,' and he does it." When Jesus heard this, he was amazed at him, and turning to the crowd following him, he said, "I tell you, I have not found such great faith even in Israel."* (Luke 7:6-9)

This centurion was a Roman army officer who had 100 soldiers under his command. From his own experience he was well aware of the power of the spoken word when delivered by someone with authority, and believed that a mere utterance by Jesus was powerful enough to heal his servant—even at a distance. Jesus was touched by the humility of this powerful man, and declared his amazement at this man's faith to the crowd.

Power is a hot topic and has been theorized about by some of the world's greatest thinkers, including Aristotle, Machiavelli, Weber, and Marx. Unraveling the mysteries of who has power, how they get it, and how they hold on to it are not easily answered—especially since those who are the most powerful seem to be the least accessible for study.

What exactly *is* power? Is it really corrupt, a disease, pathological, epidemic, and addictive? Some say it is the "ability to make something happen—or perhaps to prevent something from happening; the ability to control events, decisions, or behaviors."[21] Others define it as the capacity to produce effects on others[22] or the potential to influence.[23] Burns defines power

> ...not as a property or entity or possession, but as a relationship in which two or more persons tap motivational bases in one another and bring varying resources to bear in the process is to perceive power as drawing a vast range of human behavior into its orbit.[24]

Max Weber says power "is the probability that one actor within a social relationship will be in a position to carry out his own will despite resistance, regardless of the basis on which this probability rests."[25] There is much disagreement amongst scholars on how to define power, but as Burns believes, power may be the single most important concept in *all* the social sciences.

Power is not equivalent to leadership, but it is a necessary component of effective leadership. The potential to use power to influence is not a one-way street where the person exercising leadership is the sole power holder, using power to influence everyone else. Power is like a two-way street with an express lane down the middle that can be opened from either direction depending on the situation. The potential of using power to influence can be utilized by the leader or the collaborators. "Thus merely having the capacity to exert influence can often bring about intended effects, even though the leader may not take any action to influence his or her followers."[26]

This new understanding of leadership takes the old paradigm of power and expands it to power sharing so that it is no longer a finite entity. Burns explains the psychological conception of power as a relationship which—unlike a finite entity—can be passed around.[27] The elements of this view of power consist of "the motives and resources of the power holder; the motives and resources of power resources; and the relationship among all these."[28] Power collapses if either of these (resources or motives) is lacking.[29] It is clear that power and leadership have been affected by each others' evolution.

As discussed earlier, Jesus empowered people by sharing power with them, since his self-actualized nature freed him from the need/desire to have power *over* others. Horney says the person who seeks power is

> ...*just exactly likely to be the one who shouldn't have it, because he neurotically and compulsively needs power. Such people are apt to use power very badly; that is, use it for overcoming, overpowering, hurting people, or, to say it in other words, they use it for their own selfish gratification, conscious and unconscious, neurotic as well as healthy.... He is essentially looking out for himself, for a kind of self-cure of neurosis for a self-gratification.... The pushy people are exactly the ones who shouldn't have power. The safest person to give power to is the one who doesn't enjoy power. He is the least likely to use it for selfish, neurotic, or sadistic purposes.... If a person struggles for leadership and for bosshood, then this is one dangerous point.*[30]

Jesus motivation to practice leadership came from altruistic reasons instead of inadequacy and inferiority. He simply had power, embraced it, and used it when necessary.

Leadership Functions

Power

How do you know when to exert your power?

How are power and humility related?

What makes a person power-hungry?

What is the source of _your_ power?

What different types of power do you display?

Would it be better if you had more or less power than you do right now? Why?

Conflict

*I*t is inadequate to discuss power as exhibited in the previous vignettes without also addressing conflict. Jesus knew conflict was inevitable and was not afraid to confront it directly. In Luke 12:49-51, it is cited that Jesus exclaimed,

> *"I have come to bring fire on the earth, and how I wish it were already kindled! But I have a baptism to undergo, and how distressed I am until it is completed! Do you think I came to bring peace on earth? No, I tell you, but division."*

In order for Jesus to complete the mission for which he came, he had to understand conflict and face it. Jesus did not placate people or try to minimize the personal costs of participating in leadership with him. He admits, "For I have come to turn a man against his father, a daughter against her mother, a daughter-in-law against her mother-in-law..." *(Matthew 10:35)*. The lines were undeniably drawn: Jesus warned, "He who is not with me is against me..." *(Luke 11:23)*.

When conflict arose between the disciples, Jesus diffused the situation and brought unity to his team. An example of this occurred when the 10 disciples became enraged when James and John asked Jesus if they could sit on Jesus' right and left in heaven *(Mark 10:37)*. Jesus diffused hostile situations by reasoning that to *become great* one must really take on the role of the servant *(Mark 10:42-43)*. Jesus encouraged people to be reconciled to one another telling them to "try hard to be reconciled...." He deduced that "If a kingdom is divided against itself, that kingdom cannot stand. If a house is divided against itself, that house cannot stand" *(Mark 3:24-25)*.

Jesus maintained order and displayed a demeanor when dealing with the issue of reconciliation. He taught that

If your brother sins against you, go and show him his fault, just between the two of you. If he listens to you, you have won your brother over. But if he will not listen, take one or two others along, so that "every matter may be established by the testimony of two or three witnesses." If he refuses to listen to them, tell it to the church; and if he refuses to listen even to the church, treat him as you would a pagan or a tax collector. (Matthew 18:15-17)

Although Jesus gave this as a specific example of confrontation, he did not have one particular method for dealing with conflict. Depending on the context, Jesus used different methods. Sometimes he appeared passive toward conflict as in Matthew 26:50-51, when, as he was about to be betrayed, said to Judas, "Friend, do what you came for. Then the men stepped forward, seized Jesus and arrested him." This apparently passive behavior was completely proactive in nature. Jesus accepted what needed to be accomplished through his arrest, which made this act no less powerful than when he overturned the tables of the moneychangers and the benches of those selling doves in the temple (Matthew 21:12).

The consistency in which Jesus dealt with conflict lies in the fact that he approached it humbly and never needed to prove himself or his power to others. This is evident when Satan tempted Jesus to turn a stone into bread at the end of his 40-day fast in the desert (Luke 4:3-4). Jesus confronted this conflict with the truth and stood firm on it. This same attitude is also seen at his crucifixion when the chief priests, the teachers of the law, and the elders mocked him: "He saved others; but he can't save himself! He's the King of Israel! Let him come down now from the cross, and we will believe in him" (Matthew 27:42). Earlier, the Pharisees had challenged him to give them a sign, but he refused (Mark 8:11-13). Certainly, Jesus did not need to prove himself in these situations; he simply refused to participate in the game-playing of his adversaries.

Jesus dealt with his critics in a variety of ways, and it is probable that the technique he used most often was to ask rhetorical questions. An excellent example of this is when Jesus had returned home to Capernaum and an overflow crowd had gathered to hear him speak in a house. A group of men arrived, four of them carrying a paralytic who was lying on a mat. They were unable to get through the door for him to be healed, so they removed the center of the roof and lowered the paralyzed man down on the mat so that he was directly in front of Jesus. When Jesus said, "Son your sins are forgiven," the Pharisees and the teachers of the law who were sitting there began to think in their hearts that Jesus was blaspheming. Jesus immediately knew what they were thinking, and at this point began to ask rhetorical questions in order to reframe the situation.

> "Why are you thinking these things? Which is easier: to say to the paralytic, 'Your sins are forgiven,'" or to say, 'Get up, take your mat and walk'? But that you may know that the Son of Man has authority on earth to forgive sins...."
> He said to the paralytic, "I tell you, get up, take your mat and go home." He got up, took his mat and walked out in full view of them all. This amazed everyone and they praised God, saying, "We have never seen anything like this!"
> (Mark 2:8-12)

By using this technique of reframing the question, Jesus was able to challenge people to think radically new thoughts. Again, as shown in the example below, Jesus was able to brilliantly deflect the criticism of his adversaries by countering their question with a question when the chief priests, the teachers of the law, and the elders challenged his authority.

> "Tell us by what authority you are doing these things," they said. "Who gave you this authority?" [Jesus] replied, "I will also ask you a question. Tell me, John's baptism—was it from heaven, or from men?" They discussed it among

themselves and said, "If we say, 'From heaven,'
he will ask, 'Why didn't you believe him?' But
if we say, 'From men,' all the people will stone
us, because they are persuaded that John was a
prophet." So they answered, "We don't know
where it was from." Jesus said, "Neither will I
tell you by what authority I am doing these
things." (Luke 20:2-8)

Jesus found himself in a situation in which most people would
have reacted defensively. Instead, he turned the tables on his
opponents and challenged them to defend themselves. When
they were unable to offer a defense, Jesus was released from
any obligation to defend himself.

Another technique employed by Jesus to deal with his critics was
to confront them directly with the unblemished truth. This
technique proved very effective as the recipient of the truth was
often shocked at Jesus' candidness, and it usually disarmed their
response. When the Pharisees and Herodians tried to trap Jesus
with his own words by asking him if they should pay taxes to
Caesar, he called them on it.

"Why are you trying to trap me?" he asked.
"Bring me a denarius and let me look at it." They
brought the coin, and he asked them, "Whose
portrait is this? And whose inscription?"
"Caesar's," they replied. Then Jesus said to them,
"Give to Caesar what is Caesar's and to God
what is God's." And they were amazed at him.
(Mark 12:16-17)

Jesus was willing to point out their hypocrisy. When some
synagogue rulers criticized Jesus for healing a crippled woman
on the Sabbath, Jesus did not mince words to tell them:

You hypocrites! Doesn't each of you on the
Sabbath untie his ox or donkey from the stall and
lead it out to give it water? Then should not this
woman, a daughter of Abraham, whom Satan has

kept bound for eighteen long years, be set free on the Sabbath day from what bound her?" (Luke 13:15-16)

Another technique Jesus used to deal with critics was to cite the truth, and then point to a bigger picture of how events work together. For example, when the Pharisees asked Jesus why his disciples didn't follow the tradition of washing their hands before they ate, he showed them that they were missing the bigger picture of what it meant to follow God's commands because they were over-focusing on the details of the (Old Testament) law *(Mark 7:13)*.

At other times Jesus reasoned with his critics. When the Pharisees questioned him about divorce, Jesus explained that the reason for Moses' actions was the condition of the people's hardened hearts in this matter *(Mark 10:3-8)*. Another time, one of the teachers of the law asked him which was the most important commandment. Jesus fully explained the answer to him: "'Love the Lord your God with all your heart and with all your soul and with all your mind and with all your strength.'" The second is this: "'Love your neighbor as yourself.'" There is no commandment greater than these" *(Mark 12:30-31)*. When appropriate, Jesus took the time to reason with his critics.

Jesus moved effortlessly from adversary to adversary, artfully diffusing and deflecting each piece of criticism. He never backed down from his opponents and each and every time he was challenged, he responded humbly and powerfully. This was true even when he used the technique of silence while he was on trial *(Luke 23:8-9)*.

Managing conflict, as many believe, is how real change takes place. Maintaining the status quo is no longer held in such high esteem as it used to be. In fact, leaders like Heifetz are finding that

> *...rather than protecting people from outside threat, one lets people feel the threat in order to stimulate adaptation; instead of orienting people*

*to their current roles, one disorients people so that
new role relationships develop; rather than quelling
conflict, one generates it; instead of maintaining
norms, one challenges them.*[31]

Jesus knew the inevitability of conflict and did not seek to minimize the unpleasantness they would face in having to deal with conflict in leadership. Jesus was candid and admitted "I have come to turn a man against his father, a daughter against her mother, a daughter-in-law against her mother-in-law..." (*Matthew 10:35*). Jesus did not minimize the detriments of participating in leadership with him.

When planning how to approach a conflict, leaders and collaborators should consider the scope of the problem. Schattschneider believes "the outcome of all conflict is determined by the scope of its contagion"[32] and adds: "The best point at which to manage conflict is before it starts."[33] Deciding whether to socialize or privatize the conflict depends on the people involved and what they hope to accomplish. Changing the scope of the problem "makes possible a new pattern of competition, a new balance of forces, and a new result, but it also makes impossible a lot of other things."[34] If including the public—socializing the conflict—will enroll more people into your side than the other, it is typically more advantageous to widen the scope of the problem. Many times "it is the weak, not the strong, who appeal to public authority for relief."[35]

Jesus strategically planned when to tell his disciples information about the future and what they should expect. He also controlled conflict in a savvy way by using the context of a situation to help determine how he would respond to it and controlled the scope of the conflict by telling his disciples to not tell anyone certain information until the appointed time. Jesus dealt with conflict in many different ways: confronting conflicts head-on by stating the truth; encouraging people to be reconciled with one another; using rhetorical questions to deflect criticism; putting the bigger picture into perspective; reasoning; and, once in a while, remaining silent.

> *...it is more useful to think about a good process for handling a flow of problems than to think about "solving" a particular problem once and for all. In fluid and turbulent times it is better to think in terms of coping with conflicts than resolving them.*[36]

By not assuming that this world is rational and that every problem can have a perfect solution, we are free to take a fresh approach when looking at problems. This adds power to the process of leadership. Rather than coming to solve all the problems of the world, Jesus came to teach people to cope with the difficulties of life, such as conflict. Jesus showed people how to live a better life by being a servant and helping them to reframe their outlook on life.

Conflict

Do you tend to avoid conflict or confront it?

What's the difference between a surface argument and a root cause?

What is the meaning of the statement, "A kingdom divided against itself cannot stand"?

What is your typical approach when addressing critics and naysayers? Is it working? How do you know?

Why is a defensive posture almost always weak?

Transformational Leadership

Burns' concept of transformational leadership occurs when a leader engages "with others in such a way that leaders and followers raise one another to higher levels of motivation and morality."[37] A clear example of transformational leadership is reflected in Ford's work. He reports that

> ...because of the great paradigm shifts, which our world is undergoing..., we need both a supreme model and the source, which Jesus provides for transforming leaders—leaders, who can empower us to be more than we have been. Transforming leaders are those who are able to divest themselves of their power and invest it in their followers in such a way that others are empowered, while the leaders themselves end [up] with the greatest power of all, the power of seeing themselves reproduced in others.[38]

According to Tichy and Devanna, the key to corporate transformation and the revitalization of the American economy will be through transformational leadership.[39] Murry also claims that there is a need to "address leadership holistically, including the importance and implications of physical, emotional, and spiritual well-being of both leaders and followers."[40]

In order to raise followers to higher levels of motivation and morality, the leader must "have a clear understanding of his own values and behave consistently with them—indeed, must personify them—if his visions are to be taken seriously by others."[41] Certain characteristics, as described by Tichy and Devanna, assist the transformational leader in earning the trust and respect of their followers. These characteristics include being value-driven, courageous, an agent for change, a lifelong learner, having the ability to deal with uncertainty, ambiguity, and complexity, and truly believing in people.[42]

Gardner further extends this concept of transformational leadership by adding that morally acceptable leaders understand mutual dependence between groups and individuals, release human potential, encourage individual initiative and responsibility, and restore fundamental values.[43] It is this power to raise the level of society through the individual that sets apart the true leader from the false.

> *Historically, the greatest leaders have based their purposes on virtue, high ethical standards, and the dignity of human beings. If...leaders engage in educative acts, there must be a definition that takes into account the moral, intellectual, and spiritual development of both leaders and followers in order to determine if purposes are really mutual.*[44]

Again and again, Burns' idea of the leader as a moral agent emerges from the literature.

Burns uses the "modal values of honor and integrity; ...the end values of equality and justice; ...and the impact on the well-being of the persons whose lives were touched" as the test for authentic leadership.[45] Sashkin's theory of organizational leadership expands these criteria to encompass the *personal* characteristics of leaders—the organizational contexts in which leaders act, and the specific actions leaders take to focus on the ways in which transformational leaders empower their followers. These leaders also incorporate micro/macro integration of the leadership process.[46] These criteria are helpful in forming the dynamic of transformational leadership; however, the "leader's main strength is the ability to operate close enough to the followers to draw them up to the leader's level of moral development."[47]

Essentially, transformational leadership is concerned with the follower. Since the focus of transformational leaders is on serving their followers, it is inevitable that these followers will form a deep commitment to this relationship. Moreover, there is great societal value in investigating transformational leadership.

Transformational Leadership

Who are the people who have contributed the most to your personal transformation?

What does it mean to reproduce yourself in others?

Describe a time when you intentionally divested yourself of power. Why did you do it?

What are the implications of the belief that the mind, body, and spirit of a person are intricately connected?

How do you know when the purposes that you share with others are truly mutual?

What allows you to get close to people and subsequently influence them?

Servant Leadership

*J*esus was a servant leader; he declared that he came not to be served, but to serve others (*Matthew 20:28*). In the Bible the words "servant" and "serve" are used 1,452 times.[48] A humble heart is the foundation of a servant leader. One of the biggest points of agreement among authors who write about Jesus' leadership is his servant's attitude toward his followers (Ford,[49] Engstrom,[50] Erwin,[51] Richards & Hoeldtke,[52] Olson,[53] Jones,[54] Eims,[55] Olbricht,[56] Jordan,[57] and Boehme[58]). Erwin acknowledges that "Jesus' servanthood to the disciples made his love clear. No one had ever loved them in this wholly unselfish way.... [Servanthood is] the common thread that weaves the New Testament together."[59] And from the foundational cornerstone of humility springs this servant's attitude.[60] Boehme declares that

> *Jesus' servant leadership was perfectly manifested in his humility and brokenness of spirit. He was the most humble man who ever walked the earth.... Jesus was perfect in accountability and submission to authority. He never acted independently or with insubordination. He was always under the authority and direction of God the Father.*[61]

A humble heart is the foundation of a servant leader. Jesus distinguishes between "ruling over" others and "serving among" them in Matthew 20:25-26.[62] Self-exaltation was not part of Jesus' servant leadership model. Jones separates the glory-seekers from the true leaders by their commitment to service.[63]

Jesus "wants his followers to treat the child as they would the king, to reward any who act in his name, to sacrifice themselves for the 'little ones,' and to be at peace with one another."[64] Olson describes Jesus as one who directs the sheep, protects them, anticipates their needs and meets them, and truly loves his followers.[65] Instead of putting pressure on the masses to submit to the leaders, Jesus demanded that the leaders be the "slave of all."[66] This is a difficult task due to the fact that

> Servant leadership carries with it a high cost....
> [The leader] will seem unimpressive. He will
> suffer under misunderstanding and may be reduced
> at times to near-despair.... His gentleness itself,
> in a world where decisive and competitive men
> are admired, will lead to charges of weakness.[67]

However, servant leadership is not weak; rather, it is the strongest and most successful model.

Jesus' teaching of servant leadership was successful because his example was congruent: he never asked his followers to do something he was not willing to do first.[68] Only one time did Jesus say he was setting an example—when he washed the feet of his disciples.[69] Regarding the foot-washing, Boehme maintains that through this

> ...one act Jesus destroyed for all time any concept
> of leadership that smacks of power and position
> grabbing. He had every reason to command both
> rank and status before his disciples. But he knew
> the essence of leadership: It is service to others.
> True leadership is measured by how many people
> you serve, not how many people you control.[70]

Jones notes that nothing Jesus could have said in an attempt to teach the disciples humbleness would have been more powerful than the dramatic, acted-out parable of washing their feet.[71]

Through his servant leadership, Jesus was congruent in his speech and actions. As evidence of this congruence, Olson [72] points out that Jesus told his disciples to "Turn the other cheek," and then later did so himself when he was betrayed and arrested in the Garden of Gethsemane. The ever-zealous Peter wanted to defend Jesus with his sword, but Jesus would not allow it. Another example occurred when Jesus taught the multitudes to "Love your enemies," and then was able to pray on the cross,

"Father forgive them for they know not what they do."[73] As recorded in Matthew 23, Jesus spent 39 verses commanding his followers to do and observe what the Pharisees were instructing them to do, but not to follow their hypocritical example of *saying* things, and then not *doing* them.[74]

The focal point of Jesus' outreach was service. He served others emotionally, physically, and spiritually and had the attitude of a servant in everything he did. For example, Jesus continuously changed his schedule to better accommodate his followers' needs. There were many times when he had been traveling or teaching all day, yet he would consider people's requests instead of seeking rest or food. And he expected the same from his disciples. Jesus told them, "...any of you who does not give up everything he has cannot be my disciple" (Luke 14:33). Jesus lived a life of service to others and also required his followers to make the same sacrifice.

The cost to participate in leadership with Jesus was high. Jesus called his followers to cross conventional boundaries and reach out to people in order to meet their needs. He likened their service to others as service unto himself.

> "For I was hungry and you gave me something to eat, I was thirsty and you gave me something to drink, I was a stranger and you invited me in, I needed clothes and you clothed me, I was sick and you looked after me, I was in prison and you came to visit me." (Matthew 25:35-36)

Jesus challenged people to take the road less traveled. He taught them to get out of their comfort zone, to give and love while not expecting to receive anything in return.

He confronted their preconceived notions about leadership by telling them that the "greatest among you will be your servant" (Matthew 23:11). Jesus changed the ratings for the traditional scale of success. His proposed model of leadership was not about privilege and favor; it was about sacrifice and service.

> *An argument started among the disciples as to*
> *which of them would be the greatest. Jesus,*
> *knowing their thoughts, took a little child and*
> *had him stand beside him. Then he said to them,*
> *"Whoever welcomes this little child in my name*
> *welcomes me; and whoever welcomes me welcomes*
> *the one who sent me. For he who is least among*
> *you all—he is the greatest."* (Luke 9:46-48)

On many occasions Jesus spoke about the paradox concerning the least and the greatest. In Luke 7:28, it is noted that Jesus said, "I tell you, among those born of women there is no one greater than John; yet the one who is least in the kingdom of God is greater than he." And again, in Mark 10:42-45, Jesus is seen calling his disciples together and exhorting them to not lord their authority over others, but to be their servants. Jesus' concept of leadership was not to exert power "over" others, but to exercise power "with" others as their servant.

Boehme[75] points out that there are basically two different types of leadership. The first is characterized by *domination* over others, which operates out of the fear of losing power and seeks to have control over followers through fear and intimidation. The motives behind this kind of leadership are often based on ego needs, along with the desire for power and status. The motives that drive the desires for the second type of leadership—*servant leadership*—are much different than domination leadership. The servant leader does not seek position or status, and the followers' best interests are always of the utmost importance when considering how each of them should participate in the leadership process. Due to the servant leaders' high respect of and value for the people they serve, they do not seek to manipulate others—only to collaborate, cooperate, and empower them. Boehme elaborates:

> *The leadership of servanthood is that of example*
> *and loving persuasion.... [The] leader does not*
> *force his rule upon his people: he appeals to their*
> *hearts and minds; he sets an example by the way*

that he lives and moves; he serves them with his
gifts and his life; and in so doing, he wins their
love and respect. They follow him because they
want to follow. They grant him authority by
willing consent.[76]

Greenleaf characterizes "servant leadership" as being a servant *first*. In evaluating whether servant leadership is occurring, one should ask, "Do those served grow as persons? Do they, while being served, become healthier, wiser, freer, more autonomous, and more likely themselves to become servants?"[77] The essence of servant leadership is leading by example.

A leader initiates the ideas and the structure, and
takes the risk of failure along with the chance of
success. A leader says, "I will go; follow me!"
while knowing that the path is uncertain, even
dangerous. One then trusts those who go with
one's leadership.[78]

Just as servant leadership asks whether the followers have been served, Avolio, Waldman, and Yammarino believe that "transformational leadership is an integral part of ensuring a committed work force focused on cooperation and innovation."[79]

Servant Leadership

Recall a time when you were insulted, or "slapped."
Did you turn the other cheek? Why or why not?

What would make you become a person who <u>could</u> turn
the other cheek?

Why would someone want to serve another person
or groups of people?

How could a person be both the least of all
<u>and</u> the greatest of all?

Describe how you demonstrate the relationship between
serving and leading.

How can meeting the tangible, everyday needs of another
human being become leadership moments?
What happens if leaders don't address those needs?

Leadership through Example

$\mathcal{J}$esus used his own example as a stellar leader to help develop his followers' leadership abilities. Jesus never asked his disciples to do anything that he was not willing to do himself. Jesus did not live by a double standard; he always followed the same instructions that he gave to his disciples. Jesus chose to humble himself and be baptized as an example to others *(Luke 3:21)*. In Luke 9:5, Jesus instructed his disciples to shake the dust off their feet when people did not welcome them. And in Luke 8:26-37, it is documented that in the region of the Gerasenes (on the east shore of the Lake of Galilee), Jesus healed a demon-possessed man by casting out the many demons that were in him into a large herd of pigs, which then ran down a steep hillside into the lake and drowned. The people were overcome with fear when they heard about this and when they asked Jesus to leave, he got into the boat and left. Another time in a Samaritan village the

> *...people there did not welcome him, because he was heading for Jerusalem. When the disciples James and John saw this, they asked, "Lord, do you want us to call fire down from heaven to destroy them?" But Jesus turned and rebuked them, and they went to another village.*
> *(Luke 9:53-56)*

In one of Jesus' more challenging moments, another example is found. He held fast to his own teaching of "turning the other cheek" while he was being arrested. He could have resisted and retaliated, but he willingly allowed the soldiers to arrest him and refused to let his disciples defend him *(Luke 22:49-51)*. This is a display of tremendous discipline and shows Jesus' commitment to being a congruent example.

Jesus was a man of his word. There were no inconsistencies between his words and his actions. It is noted in Luke 24:20 that

Cleophas described Jesus as "a prophet, powerful in word and deed before God and all the people." Jesus instructed his followers to let their "yes" be "yes," and their "no," "no" (*Matthew 5:37*). Regarding the Pharisees' actions, Jesus told the crowds and his disciples

> "You must obey [the Pharisees] and do everything they tell you. But do not do what they do, for they do not practice what they preach. They tie up heavy loads and put them on men's shoulders, but they themselves are not willing to lift a finger to move them." (*Matthew 23:3-4*)

In contrast to the Pharisees, Jesus required his followers to have congruence between their actions and their words. He also made a distinction between the appearance of external righteousness and the more important matters of the heart. Jesus reprimanded the Pharisees because

> "...[you] clean the outside of the cup and dish, but inside you are full of greed and wickedness. You foolish people! Did not the one who made the outside make the inside also? But give what is inside the dish to the poor, and everything will be clean for you." (*Luke 11:39-41*)

Jesus admonished those who caused other people to sin, and had strong words for those who did not follow their own teachings. He called them "hypocrites." In Luke 6:46-48, he challenged the people with a question:

> "Why do you call me, 'Lord, Lord,' and do not do what I say? I will show you what he is like who comes to me and hears my words and puts them into practice. He is like a man building a house, who dug down deep and laid the foundation on rock. When a flood came, the torrent struck that house but could not shake it, because it was well built.

Jesus' plan to put his teaching into practice required tremendous sacrifice, but he promised great rewards to those who are wise enough to "build their house on the firm foundation."

Leading by example requires authenticity. Hitt defines authenticity as

> ...the congruence between the inner-self and the outer-self. The inner-self is the abode of your thoughts and feelings. The outer-self is manifested in your words and actions. Inner-self and outer-self will be all of a piece.[80]

Jesus was completely authentic; his outer-self and inner-self mirrored each other. Jesus lived by the same instructions that he gave his disciples. This was evident when he turned the other cheek (Luke 22:49-51), and when he left the villages that did not welcome him (Luke 9:5; Luke 8:37).

Jesus' authenticity aided him immensely in practicing leadership. His "leadership through example" approach was the most effective way to gain commitment from followers and to teach them how to practice leadership themselves. DePree proclaims, "One of the great dangers to organizations arises when a leader's private and public promises contradict each other."[81] Nair affirms that, "Your life is your message. Leadership by example is not only the most pervasive but also the most enduring form of leadership."[82] And since leadership in the postindustrial era no longer consists solely of what the leader does, this exhortation applies to everyone in the leadership process.

Certainly Jesus was authentic and practiced leadership by example. His authenticity enabled followers to feel comfortable trusting him; however, the Pharisees and teachers of the law were threatened by his authenticity. Hitt affirms this point with the comment that "The major risk in being an authentic person is that you may be a threat to some individuals.... A person who 'says it like it is' is very likely to be viewed as a threat."[83] Jesus, however, was so self-actualized that he was willing to take well-calculated risks in order to be authentic.

Leadership through Example

How are you working to re-create your own capacity for
leadership in the people around you?

Have you ever said to someone "Will you follow me?"
If so, what happened? If not, why not?

Why do you think the phrase "walking the talk"
has become so popular?

Are you a person of your word?
What determines whether or not a person is a liar?

What does the phrase "Let your 'yes' be 'yes,'
and your 'no' be 'no'" mean?

Are most people inconsistent in their behavior?

If your life is your message, what are you teaching?

Sacrifice

*P*articipating in a leadership relationship with Jesus required much sacrifice. Jesus made his expectations clear, and told his disciples that "anyone who does not take his cross and follow me is not worthy of me. Whoever finds his life will lose it, and whoever loses his life for my sake will find it" *(Matthew 10:38-39)*. The twelve Apostles gave up their careers, being near their families, and the security of a home and possessions to venture into the unknown with their teacher. He sent them out with these instructions: "Take nothing for the journey except a staff—no bread, no bag, no money in your belts. Wear sandals but not an extra tunic" *(Mark 6:8-9)*.

Jesus' followers certainly realized the risk of being involved in this movement within this radical character, since he had told them,

> *"You will be handed over to the local councils and flogged in the synagogues. On account of me you will stand before governors and kings as witnesses to them.... Brother will betray brother to death, and a father his child. Children will rebel against their parents and have them put to death. All men will hate you because of me, but he who stands firm to the end will be saved.... So be on your guard; I have told you everything ahead of time."* *(Mark 13:9-23)*

It is amazing that Jesus was able to get people to sign up to be part of his team after giving them such an "enticing" recruitment pitch. Jesus called for 100-percent devotion to the cause. He warned, "If anyone is ashamed of me and my words, the Son of Man will be ashamed of him when he comes in his glory and in the glory of the Father and of the holy angels" *(Luke 9:26)*. Yes, following Jesus required tremendous commitment and sacrifice, but he also offered a redeeming purpose for his followers by encouraging them to invest in something bigger than themselves.

Servant leadership involves much sacrifice. DePree deduces that "Leadership may be good work, but it's also a tough job."[84] Those who have not been leaders themselves often glamorize leadership. Heifetz addresses some of the sacrifices involved in being a leader, asserting that leaders "get attacked, dismissed, silenced, and sometimes assassinated.... One risks job, reputation, and perhaps life."[85] Jesus accepted these risks in order to most effectively advance his cause. What a sacrifice it was for the Apostles to give up all the security and comforts of home to embark on this precarious course with him. Jesus did not glamorize their leadership commitment; rather, he bluntly told them of the risks involved in participation (*Mark 13:9-23*).

Sacrifice

Why would people want to make sacrifices?

Has anyone ever made a significant sacrifice for you?

Is sacrifice consistent with your culture or subculture?

*What's the difference between being a risk-taker
and someone who is willing to sacrifice?*

*Have you ever chosen to let go of something truly precious?
What happened?*

Purpose

Jesus' purpose was not to "preach all the sermons, do all the miracles, right all the wrongs, or solve all the problems. His purpose was to reproduce the life he had in himself from his Father, to re-create his own leadership in his chosen people."[86] Jesus understood his purpose and cleaved to his mission. For example, in Mark 1:38, Jesus said to Simon and his companions, "Let us go somewhere else—to the nearby villages—so I can preach there also. That is why I have come." Jesus knew the truth and used it to keep himself focused on his mission. After Satan had tempted Jesus for forty days in the desert wilderness, he led him to the highest point of the temple in Jerusalem and challenged him to throw himself down to prove that the angels would protect him. Jesus answered by quoting Scriptures: "Do not put the Lord your God to the test" (Luke 4:9-12). Jesus also stated his mission in order to stay on task when the people of Galilee tried to keep him from leaving them: "...I must preach the good news of the kingdom of God to the other towns also, because that is why I was sent" (Luke 4:42-43). Jesus knew exactly why and to whom he had been sent. He claimed he was sent for the lost sheep of Israel (Matthew 15:24), to "heal the sick, raise the dead, cleanse those who have leprosy, drive out demons..." (Matthew 10:8), and to call "sinners to repentance" (Luke 5:32). Jesus made it clear that he "did not come to be served, but to serve, and to give his life as a ransom for many" (Matthew 20:28). Jesus came to improve peoples' lives, and told them "...I have come that they may have life, and have it to the full" (John 10:10). He also knew that he had come to set people free, and asserted that

> "The Spirit of the Lord is on me, because he has anointed me to preach good news to the poor. He has sent me to proclaim freedom for the prisoners and recovery of sight for the blind, to release the oppressed, to proclaim the year of the Lord's favor." (Luke 4:18-19)

The freedom that he spoke of was freedom from sin and bondage; he came not to abolish the law, but to fulfill it *(Matthew 5:17)*.

Jesus shared his vision with his followers. He eventually commissioned them to

> *"Therefore go and make disciples of all nations, baptizing them in the name of the Father and of the Son and of the Holy Spirit, and teaching them to obey everything I have commanded you. And surely I am with you always, to the very end of the age."* (Matthew 28:19-20)

Jesus' compelling purpose was also actualized through his vision for the future.

Frankyl claims that searching for meaning and purpose is at the essence of humanity. He suggests that meaning is discovered through a person's actions, sufferings, achievements, and love.[87] Channon also affirms the importance of "knowing the meaning of the corporation's purpose in the world and having a tangible 'experience' of that purpose [which] constitutes *esprit de corps* for the employees. *Esprit de corps* is a sense of ownership in the corporate enterprise,"[88] and is a critical component in helping to motivate the staff. Channon adds that

> *Belonging to a group, especially a group that is making a difference in the world can be a powerful motivating factor. People who know they are working for something larger with a more noble purpose can be expected to be loyal and dependable and, at minimum, more inspired.*[89]

Jesus provided an opportunity for people to be part of a group that had a clear purpose and a powerful motivating vision.

Having a purpose when practicing leadership also provides many advantages for the leaders and followers. Heifetz claims that, "Preserving a sense of purpose helps one take setbacks and failures in stride. Leadership requires the courage to face failures daily.... A sense of purpose provides the ongoing capacity to generate new possibilities."[90] Purpose is truly the backbone of keeping an organization on track and motivated in difficult circumstances. Without purpose, Heifetz acknowledges that

> ...the emotions of leadership...can overwhelm the person who has not developed a sufficiently broad sense of purpose.... The practice of leadership requires, perhaps first and foremost, a sense of purpose—the capacity to find the values that make risk-taking meaningful.[91]

Starratt challenges institutions to articulate their purposes and then to compare their purposes to the practices of the institution.[92] Holding an organization accountable to its purposes is a higher standard that can only benefit the organization. Smith suggests that "we can raise the level of purpose by working toward broad ideals and widely shared needs over time. Working on mission statements or envisioning desirable futures are ways we do that."[93] Part of envisioning a desirable future requires a decision as to which direction to take in order to fulfill the purpose. Many times the purpose is translated into a vision, which we will discuss in the next chapter.

Purpose

What is the purpose for your life?
If you don't know, what steps could you take to find out?

Who is one person you know that has clarity of purpose?
How did they figure out their purpose in life?

How will the world be better because of your existence?

Describe what it's like to work for or with someone who has no clarity of purpose

Vision

Jesus had a vision for the future and lived according to the mission that would fulfill that vision. The vision that Jesus possessed was not full of grandiose hype: it was useful and realistic. One vision Jesus had was in Luke 10:18, after the seventy-two followers had returned from being sent out ahead of him. Jesus related that he "saw Satan fall like lightning from heaven." Another occurred at Jesus' baptism when he "saw heaven being torn open and the Spirit descending on him like a dove. And a voice came from heaven: 'You are my son whom I love; with you I am well pleased'" (Mark 1:10-11). And in Matthew 17:2-3—when Jesus was transfigured before Peter, James, and John—Moses and Elijah appeared before them, talking with Jesus. Jesus used his vision to prepare his disciples for the future. In Matthew 17:12-13, Jesus is cited as saying to his disciples

> "But I tell you, Elijah has already come, and they did not recognize him, but have done to him everything they wished. In the same way the Son of Man is going to suffer at their hands." Then the disciples understood that he was talking to them about John the Baptist.

Sharing his vision and planning for the future were integral components in preparing others to lead his cause.

The vision that helps actualize the purpose contributes to an even greater sense of meaning for the people involved in the leadership process. "Leaders who effectively communicate meaning draw on past experience, present opportunities, scenarios of the future, fundamental values, and cultural traditions to articulate inspiring visions of their organization's future."[94] Jesus' vision of the final judgment drew on previous choices from the past, as when his followers chose whether or not to feed the hungry and tend to the sick and less fortunate (Matthew 25:32-33). This also served to encourage them to serve others, as this was a determining factor in separating the "sheep from the goats."

Jesus used vision to motivate not only himself, but also the other leaders and followers in his movement. Vision and commitment are critical "to turn an organization around—to revitalize it, make it more flexible, innovative, and competitive." It is not enough to have good management, resources, and strategic planning.[95] Vision is what motivates the leader.

> *Vision is always out in front of the leader, in one sense.... The leader's vision is what motivates him, ...what enables him...to articulate the major themes of the drama in the role as director. The vision enables the leader/director to see the unity within the various scenes and subplots in the drama, and to call the various actors to express, in their own parts, those overarching themes.*[96]

Vision

What purpose does a "vision" serve?

Why do you think visioning has become such a popular practice?

What do you do if you're not a visionary and don't seem to have a vision?

What will happen to the people if there is no vision? What will happen to you?

Planning

Jesus took great care to plan ahead. Sometimes he sent forerunners to prepare the people before he arrived. One such forerunner was John the Baptist (Mark 1:4-5). At another time, in Mark 6:45, Jesus is seen sending out his disciples ahead of him: "Immediately Jesus made his disciples get into the boat and go on ahead of him to Bethsaida, while he dismissed the crowd." Jesus understood the power of strategizing his movements.

Once Jesus' ministry blossomed, he became so sought after that it was cumbersome for him to move in and out of cities. Because of this problem, he told many people to keep quiet regarding his whereabouts (Luke 5:13-15). When people spoke "freely, spreading the news...Jesus could no longer enter a town openly but stayed outside in lonely places. Yet the people still came to him from everywhere" (Mark 1:45). At times he told his disciples to "have a small boat ready for him, to keep the people from crowding him" (Mark 3:9).

Jesus instructed and prepared the disciples to deal with different situations in which they would eventually find themselves. Before he sent them out on their first internship, he gave them detailed instructions not only about what to take, but also how to deal with discouragement (Mark 6:8-11). Jesus prepared his staff for the future by telling them what to expect. On the way to Jerusalem, Jesus

> ...took the Twelve aside and told them what was going to happen to him. "We are going up to Jerusalem," he said, "and the Son of Man will be betrayed to the chief priests and teachers of the law. They will condemn him to death and will hand him over to the Gentiles, who will mock him and spit on him, flog him and kill him. Three days later he will rise." (Mark 10:32-34)

Jesus did not temper the truth. He told them all the unpleasant details so that they would be prepared for whatever came up.

Each move that Jesus made was well calculated. When Jesus and his disciples were coming down the mountain, he "gave them orders not to tell anyone what they had seen until the Son of Man had risen from the dead. They kept the matter to themselves, discussing what 'rising from the dead' meant" (Mark 9:9-10). Jesus understood the importance of timing in matters and strategized accordingly.

Jesus cautioned his followers. He told them to be on guard, to watch out, to be ready, and not to be deceived.

> ♦ *You must be on your guard.* (Mark 13:9)

> ♦ *Watch out for false prophets. They come to you in sheep's clothing, but inwardly they are ferocious wolves.* (Matthew 7:15)

> ♦ *You also must be ready, because the Son of Man will come at an hour when you do not expect him.* (Luke 12:40)

> ♦ *Watch out that no one deceives you.* (Mark 13:5)

Jesus even told them the parable of the ten virgins to encourage them to be ready:

> "At that time the kingdom of heaven will be like ten virgins who took their lamps and went out to meet the bridegroom. Five of them were foolish and five were wise. The foolish ones took their lamps but did not take any oil with them. The wise, however, took oil in jars along with their lamps. The bridegroom was a long time in coming, and they all became drowsy and fell asleep. At midnight the cry rang out: 'Here's the bridegroom! Come out to meet him!' Then all the virgins woke

up and trimmed their lamps. The foolish ones said to the wise, 'Give us some of your oil; our lamps are going out.' 'No,' they replied, 'there may not be enough for both us and you. Instead, go to those who sell oil and buy some for yourselves.' But while they were on their way to buy the oil, the bridegroom arrived. The virgins who were ready went in with him to the wedding banquet. And the door was shut." (Matthew 25:1-10)

Jesus used this parable to illustrate both the importance of being prepared and the possibility of missing out when one's priorities are not in order.

If purpose is like the pulse of an organization, the vision is like the plasma and the plans are like veins that allow circulation. Without plans and purpose the vision cannot come to fruition. Jesus carefully considered each situation before making a decision. He looked at the context instead of following a rigid set of rules. He planned everything from keeping quiet about his whereabouts (Luke 5:16), to the appointed time when he would tell his disciples about the events to come (Mark 8:30-31). Jesus planned for the long term, preparing his disciples for their internships (Mark 6:8-11), and also preparing them for the time after his resurrection when he would not be with them (Matthew 24:3-8).

Unlike Jesus, many traditional organizations believe that short-term planning is the only way they can compete with postindustrial organizations: yet short-term planning with out long-term planning inevitably leads to downsizing and liquidating. This myopic focus causes implosion, and "little can be done to stop the process, once implosion is underway in a company."[97] Some companies appear to be taking steps toward becoming postindustrial organizations, since they are using politically correct buzzwords and the latest models of management and leadership. But unfortunately, many times political correctness only masks deeper attitudinal problems within a company and can actually make it harder to get to the true crux of the problem. Oftentimes when unfamiliarity arises, the bright light of innovative leadership fades into old-style management, which is then translated into maintaining the status quo. Questions are then logically raised as to how beneficial these *misguided* steps have been toward achieving the desired postindustrial paradigm.

Substantive change requires great strategizing. Knowing how to set the agenda, and even "keeping issues that would be inconvenient off the agenda is at least as important for political success as winning disputes that do arise."[98] Building coalitions and persuading players to come over to "your side" to create "our side" is paramount to this process. Figuring out what others' priorities and perceptions are helps open the gate to uniting coalitions and building a more powerful entity. "Players" take a stand on an issue according to their stake in the matter.[99] Using the appropriate action channel is crucial to maximizing and expanding this power.

Jesus dazzled his audiences with his political savvy. When he wanted to do something for which he knew he would be scrutinized, he first set up the situation in a way that would keep it off the agenda *(Mark 3:1-5)*. Jesus also believed that collaboration was important, since he had corrected John for trying to stop a man who was driving out demons in Jesus' name *(Luke 9:49-50)*. Jesus' polytrophic response considers some of these political issues such as understanding others' priorities (stakes), meeting each person where they are at (stand), and using the appropriate response or mode of communication (action channel) to influence them.

Planning

Do leaders with faith need to plan? Why or why not?

Do you prefer to give detailed instructions
or provide more global inspiration?
What are the strengths and pitfalls of each approach?

Does your organization engage in more short-term or
long-term planning? Why?

Have you ever withheld unpleasant details from someone?
Why? What were the consequences?

Priorities

Jesus focused on worthy pursuits and encouraged others to do the same. With Jesus' plan there was no room for ill-defined or poorly managed priorities: he called his followers to a higher standard. Jesus used the situation with Mary and Martha as a lesson in prioritizing.

> *But Martha was distracted by all the preparations that had to be made. She came to him and asked, "Lord, don't you care that my sister has left me to do the work by myself? Tell her to help me!" "Martha, Martha," the Lord answered, "you are worried and upset about many things, but only one thing is needed. Mary has chosen what is better, and it will not be taken away from her."*
> (Luke 10:40-42)

Jesus carefully considered each situation before making a decision. He looked at the context instead of following a rigid set of rules. Jesus encouraged his followers to keep their priorities straight and to invest their time in things that really matter. Jesus told them

> *"Do not store up for yourselves treasures on earth, where moth and rust destroy, and where thieves break in and steal. But store up for yourselves treasures in heaven, where moth and rust do not destroy, and where thieves do not break in and steal. For where your treasure is, there your heart will be also."* (Matthew 6:19-21)

Jesus taught others about the value of discipline in priorities. In Matthew 6:33, Jesus called his followers to "seek first his kingdom, and his righteousness, and all these things will be given to you as well." Jesus also used a dramatic metaphor about letting things get in your way: "And if your eye causes you to sin, pluck it out. It is better for you to enter the kingdom of God with one eye than to have two eyes and be thrown into hell" *(Mark 9:47)*. Jesus' priorities called for complete commitment to the cause. One disciple said to him, "Lord, first let me go and bury my father." But Jesus told him, "Follow me, and let the dead bury their own dead" *(Matthew 8:21-22)*.

Jesus organized his life according to his priorities. His priorities were based *in toto* on serving his father and in serving others, not on self-interest. Mollner points out that in the

> ...Material Age worldview each person has a different top priority from everyone else; the top priority of each person at all times is his or her own self-interest. Whereas, with the Relationship Age worldview all people and things have the same top priority at all times—the good of the one whole. It is this that allows for continuous peace rather than conflict within relationships.[100]

Surely, this concept of the "good of the whole" has a long way to go before it displaces the climate of self-interest that is so well-embedded in our American culture.

DePree claims that it is the responsibility of the leader to "make sure that priorities are set, that they are steadfastly communicated and adhered to in practice."[101] Covey also acknowledges the importance of priorities and deduces that "the best thinking in the area of time management can be captured in a single phrase: Organize and execute around priorities."[102] Jesus encouraged people to concentrate their energy on matters more important than mundane monetary pursuits *(Matthew 6:19-21)*. Jesus carefully evaluated each situation and based his priorities on higher moral reasoning.

Priorities

Analyze how you spend your time.
Are your actions consistent with what you say you value?
Why or why not?

What do you treasure? Why?

Do you have many competing priorities?
What criteria will you use to sort them out?

What importance do you place on quietness and solitude?

Describe the last time you chose to be still.
What did you feel and learn?

A Higher Standard

*J*esus did more than teach others to aspire to a higher standard; he lived by the same higher standard that he set for others. Jesus many times spoke about light (or truth) exposing concealed matters. He lived his life in the light, and had nothing to hide. As discussed earlier, Jesus created an atmosphere of openness to facilitate trust. He encouraged others to "let your light shine before men, that they may see your good deeds and praise your Father in heaven" (Matthew 5:16). Jesus asked this question:

> "Do you bring in a lamp to put it under a bowl or a bed? Instead, don't you put it on its stand? For whatever is hidden is meant to be disclosed, and whatever is concealed is meant to be brought out into the open. If anyone has ears to hear, let him hear." (Mark 4:21-23)

Jesus encouraged his followers by telling them, "You are the light of the world. A city on a hill cannot be hidden" (Matthew 5:14).

Jesus required his followers to step out of their comfort zone. He told them it was not enough to simply treat people nicely who treated them well. Jesus set a higher standard of behavior with the following instructions:

> "You have heard that it was said, 'Love your neighbor and hate your enemy.' But I tell you: Love your enemies and pray for those who persecute you, that you may be sons of your Father in heaven. He causes his sun to rise on the evil and the good, and sends rain on the righteous and the unrighteous. If you love those who love you, what reward will you get? Are not even the tax collectors doing that? And if you greet only your brothers, what are you doing more than others?

Do not even pagans do that? Be perfect, therefore,
as your heavenly Father is perfect."
(Matthew 5:43-48)

It is hard to imagine a standard higher than "Be perfect, as your heavenly father is perfect." Jesus laid out the measuring stick as he instructed them to

"Be merciful, just as your Father is merciful. Do
not judge, and you will not be judged. Do not
condemn, and you will not be condemned. Forgive,
and you will be forgiven. Give, and it will be
given to you. A good measure, pressed down,
shaken together and running over, will be poured
into your lap. For with the measure you use, it
will be measured to you." (Luke 6:36-38)

This simple rule is an extraordinary concept that is woven through the heart of Jesus' message. Jesus called his followers to have "a noble and good heart, [to] hear the word, retain it, and by persevering produce a crop" (Luke 8:15). Participating in leadership with Jesus was a challenging course for one's life and required a single standard of conduct.

Unethical behavior has become a crisis domestically and internationally, and many businesses—as well as governments— are hiring consultants to teach ethics to employees and legislators. Rost breaks down the ethics in leadership into process and content, and challenges those involved in the leadership relationship to be ethical in both.[103] Nair makes this important point: "We have come to accept that a lower moral standard is necessary to get things done in the real world of politics and business. This is the gospel of expediency—the double standard of conduct."[104] In reality, "we lose respect for our leaders if we do not approve of their conduct public or private. Leaders who do not command our respect reduce the legitimacy of their leadership and lose our trust."[105]

Jesus earned the respect of his followers by proving to be congruent in his speech and actions. He called his followers to be the light of the world (Matthew 5:14), and to shun secrecy and embrace openness (Mark 4:21-23). A few of Jesus' higher standards included principles such as loving those who are difficult to love (Matthew 5:43-44), and being merciful, giving, and not judging or condemning (Luke 6:36-38).

A Higher Standard

What will happen to your enemies if you bless them?
What will happen to you?

Do you see public and private behavior as
separate and distinct realms?

Do you think most nations make a distinction between
public and private actions? Why or why not?

Do you believe a lower moral standard is necessary to
"get things done" in business today?

How would organizations be different if leaders
refused to lower their standards?

What are the societal, organizational,
and individual by-products of relativism?

Forgiveness

A major theme in Jesus' message was forgiveness. The golden rule also applied to forgiveness as Jesus reminded his followers that "when you stand praying, if you hold anything against anyone, forgive him, so that your Father in heaven may forgive you your sins" *(Mark 11:25)*. To participate in this leadership relationship with Jesus, forgiveness was mandatory. Jesus told his disciples, "If your brother sins, rebuke him, and if he repents, forgive him. If he sins against you seven times in a day, and seven times comes back to you and says, 'I repent,' forgive him" *(Luke 17:3-4)*.

Jesus used a story about a king who settled accounts with his servants to explain what the kingdom of heaven is like. After the king cancelled the debt of the servant who owed him the most, that servant went out and

> ...*found one of his fellow servants who owed him a hundred denarii. He grabbed him and began to choke him. "Pay back what you owe me!" he demanded. Then the master called the servant in. "You wicked servant," he said, "I cancelled all that debt of yours because you begged me to. Shouldn't you have had mercy on your fellow servant just as I had on you?" In anger his master turned him over to the jailers to be tortured, until he should pay back all he owed. "This is how my heavenly Father will treat each of you unless you forgive your brother from your heart."* (Matthew 18:28, 32-35)

What an effective story Jesus used to get his point across about forgiveness! Jesus deduced that people who are forgiven much will love much; and those who are forgiven little will love little *(Luke 7:47)*. The call to this higher standard of forgiveness may be challenging; however, the benefits for the forgiver are immeasurable.

Hwang proclaims that "Forgiveness is...the means to resolving many relationship conflicts involving: race, gender, family, and work-related confrontations. The ability to forgive and the willingness to let go and move on can be a very liberating ingredient...."[106] Covey avers that principle-centered leaders "forgive themselves and others. They don't condemn themselves for every foolish mistake or social blunder. They forgive others of their trespasses."[107] Starratt links forgiveness to compassion and calls for the postmodern leader to embrace both.

> [This]...does not mean rationalizing or excusing human weakness. It means, rather, the courage to name it, and then forgive it, and then to get on with the task again. Compassion means the ability to forgive because one knows one's own need for forgiveness.[108]

Forgiveness appears to be a revolutionary concept for the twenty-first century leader; however, for Jesus it was a pillar in his practice of leadership centuries ago.

Forgiveness

What is the difference between telling someone you are sorry versus asking for his or her forgiveness?

Is forgetting the same as forgiving?

Identify one person who needs to be forgiven and forgive them. Ask one person for forgiveness. Describe what you felt and what you learned.

Have you ever forgiven yourself?

If you can't have compassion on yourself, is it possible to feel compassion for others?

What has been will be again,

what has been done will be done again;

there is nothing new under the sun.

Is there anything of which one can say,

"Look! This is something new"?

It was here already, long ago;

it was here before our time.

(Ecclesiastes 1:9-10)

FINIS.

(Endnotes)

[1] Jones, L.B. (1995). *Jesus CEO: Using Ancient Wisdom for Visionary Leadership.* New York: Hyperion.

[2] Ibid.

[3] McKenna, D.L. (1989). *Power to Follow Grace to Lead.* Dallas: Word Publishing.

[4] Ibid.

[5] Ibid.

[6] Jones, L.B. (1995). *Jesus CEO: Using Ancient Wisdom for Visionary Leadership.* New York: Hyperion.

[7] Ford, L. (1991). Transforming Leadership: Jesus' Way of Creating Vision, Shaping Values, and Empowering Change. Downers Grove, IL: InterVarsity, p. 102.

[8] Ibid.

[9] Ford, L. (1991). *Transforming Leadership: Jesus' Way of Creating Vision, Shaping Values, and Empowering Change.* Downers Grove, IL: InterVarsity.

[10] McKenna, D.L. (1989). *Power to Follow Grace to Lead.* Dallas: Word Publishing.

[11] Ibid., p. 164.

[12] McKenna, D.L. (1989). *Power to Follow Grace to Lead.* Dallas: Word Publishing.

[13] Ford, L. (1991). *Transforming Leadership: Jesus' Way of Creating Vision, Shaping Values, and Empowering Change.* Downers Grove, IL: InterVarsity, p. 265-266.

[14] McKenna, D.L. (1989). *Power to Follow Grace to Lead.* Dallas: Word Publishing.

[15] Ibid., p. 134.

[16] Stephan, E., & Pace, W. (1990). *The Perfect Leader: Following Christ's Example to Leadership Success.* Salt Lake City: Deseret Book.

[17] Youssef, M. (1986). *The Leadership Style of Jesus.* Wheaton, IL: Victor Books.

[18] Ibid.

[19] Jordan, J.P. (1990). *Secular and Presbyterian Philosophies of Leadership as Compared with the Teaching and Example of Jesus Christ.* Doctoral dissertation, San Francisco Theological Seminary, p. 136.

[20] Ibid.

[21] Troustine, P., Christensen, T. (1982). *Movers and Shakers: The Study of Community Power.* New York: St. Martin's.

[22] House, R.J. (1984). *Power in Organizations: A Social Psychological Perspective.* Unpublished manuscript, University of Toronto, Canada.

[23] Bass (1990). *Bass and Stogdill's Handbook of Leadership* (3rd edition.). New York: Free Press.

[24] Burns, J.M. (1977). *Leadership*. New York: Harper & Row, p. 15.

[25] Weber, M. (1957). *The Theory of Social and Economic Organization*. Glencoe, Il: Freepress, p. 152.

[26] Hughes, R.L., Ginnett, R. C., & Curphy, G. J. (1993). *Leadership: Enhancing the Lessons of Experience*. Boston: Irwin, p. 111.

[27] Burns, J.M. (1977). *Leadership*. New York: Harper & Row.

[28] Ibid., p. 13.

[29] Ibid.

[30] Horney, K. (1937). *The Neurotic Personality of our Time*. New York: Norton, p. 125-126.

[31] Heifetz, R.A. (1994). *Leadership Without Easy Answers*. Cambridge, MA: Harvard University Press, p. 126.

[32] Schattschneider, E. (1960). *The Semisovereign People*. Hinsdale, IL: Dryden Press, p. 2.

[33] Ibid., p. 15.

[34] Ibid., p. 17.

[35] Schattschneider, E. (1960). *The Semisovereign People*. Hinsdale, IL: Dryden Press, p. 40.

[36] Fisher, R., Kopelman, E., & Schneider, A.K. (1994). *Beyond Machiavelli*. Cambridge, MA: Harvard University Press, p. 4.

[37] Burns, J.M. (1977). *Leadership*. New York: Harper & Row, p. 20.

[38] Ford, L. (1991). *Transforming Leadership: Jesus' Way of Creating Vision, Shaping Values, and Empowering Change*. Downers Grove, IL: InterVarsity, p. 15.

[39] Tichy, N.M., & Devanna, M.A. (1986). *The Transformational Leader*. New York: John Wiley & Sons.

[40] Murry, J. (1992). *Transformational Leadership*. Unpublished manuscript, The Union Institute, San Diego, CA, p. 9.

[41] Nanus, B. (1989). *The Leader's Edge*. Chicago: Contemporary Books, p. 65.

[42] Tichy, N.M., & Devanna, M.A. (1986). *The Transformational Leader*. New York: John Wiley & Sons.

[43] Gardner, J.W. (1990). *On leadership*. New York: Free Press.

[44] Murry, J. (1992). *Transformational Leadership*. Unpublished manuscript, The Union Institute, San Diego, CA.

[45] Burns, J.M. (1977). *Leadership*. New York: Harper & Row, p. 426.

[46] Sashkin, M., & Burke, W.W. (1990). *Understanding and Assessing Organizational leadership*. In K. Clark & M. Clark (Eds.), *Measures of Leadership*. West Orange, NJ: Leadership Library of America.

[47] Burns, J.M. (1977). *Leadership*. New York: Harper & Row, p. 78.

[48] Boehme, R. (1989). *Leadership for the 21st Century: Changing Nations Through the Power of Serving*. Seattle: Frontline Communications.

[49] Ford, L. (1991). *Transforming Leadership*. Downers Grove, IL: InterVarsity.

[50] Engstrom, T.W. (1976). *The Making of a Christian Leader*. Grand Rapids, MI: Zondervan.

[51] Erwin, G.D. (1988). *The Jesus Style*. Dallas: Word Publishing, p. 31.

[52] Richards, L.O., & Hoeldtke, C. (1980). *Church Leadership: Following the Example of Jesus Christ*. Grand Rapids, MI: Zondervan.

[53] Olson, H. (1991). *Power Strategies of Jesus Christ: Principles of Leadership From the Greatest Motivator of All Time*. Tarrytown, New York: Triumph books.

[54] Jones, L.B. (1995). *Jesus CEO: Using Ancient Wisdom for Visionary Leadership*. New York: Hyperion.

[55] Eims, L. (1975). *Be the Leader You Were Meant to Be*. Wheaton, Il: Victor Books.

[56] Olbricht, T.H. (1979). *The Power to Be*. Fort Worth, TX: Sweet Publishing.

[57] Jordan, J.P. (1990). *Secular and Presbyterian Philosophies of Leadership as Compared with the Teaching and Example of Jesus Christ*. Doctoral dissertation, San Francisco Theological Seminary.

[58] Boehme, R. (1989). *Leadership for the 21st Century: Changing Nations Through the Power of Serving*. Seattle: Frontline Communications.

[59] Erwin, G.D. (1988). *The Jesus Style*. Dallas: Word Publishing, p. 31.

[60] Boehme, R. (1989). *Leadership for the 21st century: Changing Nations Through the Power of Serving*. Seattle: Frontline Communications.

[61] Ibid., p. 211.

[62] Richards, L.O., & Hoeldtke, C. (1980). *Church Leadership: Following the Example of Jesus Christ*. Grand Rapids, MI: Zondervan.

[63] Jones, L.B. (1995). *Jesus CEO: Using Ancient Wisdom for Visionary Leadership*. New York: Hyperion.

[64] Ford, L. (1991). *Transforming Leadership: Jesus' Way of Creating Vision, Shaping Values, and Empowering change*. Downers Grove, IL: InterVarsity, p. 147.

[65] Olson, H. (1991). *Power Strategies of Jesus Christ: Principles of Leadership from the Greatest Motivator of All Time*. Tarrytown, New York: Triumph Books.

[66] Erwin, G.D. (1988). *The Jesus Style*. Dallas: Word publishing.

[67] Richards, L.O., & Hoeldtke, C. (1980). *Church Leadership: Following the Example of Jesus Christ*. Grand Rapids, MI: Zondervan, p. 109.

[68] Erwin, G.D. (1988). *The Jesus Style*. Dallas: Word Publishing.

[69] Ford, L. (1991). *Transforming Leadership: Jesus' Way of Creating Vision, Shaping Values, and Empowering Change*. Downers Grove, IL: InterVarsity.

[70] Boehme, R. (1989). *Leadership For the 21st Century: Changing Nations Through the Power of Serving*. Seattle: Frontline Communications, p. 216-217.

[71] Jones, L.B. (1995). *Jesus CEO: Using Ancient Wisdom for Visionary Leadership.* New York: Hyperion.

[72] Olson, H. (1991). *Power Strategies of Jesus Christ: Principles of Leadership From the Greatest Motivator of All Time.* Tarrytown, New York: Triumph books.

[73] Ibid.

[74] Jordan, J.P. (1990). *Secular and Presbyterian Philosophies of Leadership as Compared with the Teaching and Example of Jesus Christ.* Doctoral dissertation, San Francisco Theological Seminary.

[75] Boehme, R. (1989). *Leadership For the 21st Century: Changing Nations Through the Power of Serving.* Seattle: Frontline Communications.

[76] Ibid., p. 61.

[77] Greenleaf, R.K. (1977). *Servant Leadership.* New York: Paulist Press, p. 13-14.

[78] Ibid., p. 15.

[79] Avolio, B., Waldman, D., & Yammarino, F. (1990). *Leading in the 1990s: The Four I's of Transformational Leadership. Journal of European Industrial Training, 14* (4), p. 16.

[80] Hitt, W.D. (1993). *The Model Leader: A Fully Functioning Person.* Columbus, OH: Battelle Press, p. 145.

[81] DePree, M. (1992). *Leadership Jazz.* New York: Doubleday, p. 20.

[82] Nair, K. (1994). *A Higher Standard of Leadership.* San Francisco: Jossey-Bass, p. 140.

[83] Hitt, W.D. (1993). *The Model Leader: A Fully Functioning Person.* Columbus, OH: Battelle Press, p. 147.

[84] DePree, M. (1992). *Leadership Jazz.* New York: Doubleday, p. 29.

[85] Heifetz, R.A. (1994). *Leadership Without Easy Answers.* Cambridge, MA: Harvard University Press, p. 236.

[86] Ford, L. (1991). *Transforming Leadership: Jesus' Way of Creating Vision, Shaping Values, and Empowering Change.* Downers Grove, IL: InterVarsity, p. 200.

[87] Corey, G. (1991). *Theory and Practice of Counseling and Psychotherapy.* Pacific Grove, CA: Brooks/Cole.

[88] Renesch, J. (Ed.). (1995). *New Traditions in Business.* San Francisco: Berrett-Koehler, p. 53.

[89] Ibid., p. 58.

[90] Heifetz, R. A. (1994). *Leadership Without Easy Answers.* Cambridge, MA: Harvard University Press, p. 275.

[91] Ibid., p. 274.

[92] Starratt, R. J. (1993). *The Drama of Leadership.* Washington, D. C.: Falmer Press.

[93] Weisbord, M.R. (1992). *Discovering Common Ground: How Future Search Conferences Bring People Together to Achieve Breakthrough Innovation, Empowerment, Shared Vision, and Collaborative Action.* San Francisco: Berrett-Koehler, p. 175.

[94] Bryson, J.M., & Crosby, B.C. (1992). *Leadership for the Common Good: Tackling Public Problems in a Shared-Power World.* San Francisco: Jossey-Bass, p. 48.

[95] Tracey, W.R. (1990). *Leadership Skills: Standout Performance for Human Resources Managers.* New York: AMACOM, p. 132.

[96] Starratt, R.J. (1993). *The Drama of Leadership.* Washington, D.C.: Falmer Press, p. 145.

[97] Maynard, H.B. & Mehrtens, S.E. (1993). *The Fourth Wave: Business in the 21st Century.* San Francisco: Berrett-Koehler, p. 71.

[98] Lindblom, C. & Woodhouse E. (1993). *The Policy-Making Process.* Englewood Cliffs, New Jersey: Prentice Hall, p. 11.

[99] Allison, G.T. (1971). *Essence of Decision.* Boston: Little, Brown.

[100] Renesch, J. (Ed.). (1995). *New Traditions in Business.* San Francisco: Berrett-Koehler, p. 99.

[101] DePree, M. (1992). *Leadership Jazz.* New York: Doubleday, p. 29.

[102] Covey, S.R. (1990). *The 7 Habits of Highly Effective People.* New York: Simon & Schuster, p. 149.

[103] Rost, J. (1991). *Leadership for the Twenty-First Century.* New York: Praeger.

[104] Nair, K. (1994). *A Higher Standard of Leadership.* San Francisco: Jossey-Bass, p. 13.

[105] Ibid., p. 14.

[106] Hwang, P.O. (1995). *Other Esteem: A Creative Response to a Society Obsessed with Promoting the Self.* San Diego, CA: Black Forrest Press, p. 144

[107] Covey, S.R. (1989). *Principle-Centered Leadership: Teaching People How to Fish.* Provo, UT: Executive Excellence, p. 167.

[108] Starratt, R.J. (1993). *The Drama of Leadership.* Washington, D. C.: Falmer Press, p. 108.

Dr. Mays' consulting experience has focused on leadership, change management, and team-related issues. She is a personal coach and mediator with experience in organizations as well as the California Superior and Small Claims Courts. She has served Fortune 500 clients as a Senior Organizational Change Consultant for a technology consulting firm.

Presently, she is a faculty member in a Doctoral program in Organizational Leadership. Dr. Mays is the author of the book, *Courteous Rebel: Jesus' Model of Leadership*. Angie Mays received her Doctoral degree in Leadership from the University of San Diego. She also received her Master's degree in Counseling from the University of San Diego and a Bachelor's degree in Psychology from Westmont College. She has studied abroad as a graduate and undergraduate in Asia and Western Europe.

Beyond her credentials she is passionate about encouraging others and being a catalyst to help people clarify and fulfill their dreams and goals. In her free time she enjoys traveling, Viennese waltzing, swing dancing, and boating.

Dr. Cecil oversees the Organizational Leadership Program at Chapman University, San Diego, instructing graduate and undergraduate students. Previously, she served as a senior operational leader for Children's Hospital San Diego and prior to that, as the Executive Vice President of   a non-profit organization.

Christine is married with three children. Her husband Darren is an internationally recognized speaker on disability issues.

Christine has developed and delivered numerous training and coaching programs for civic leaders, community-based organizations and corporations. Her encouragement to every reader is to develop a personal relationship with Jesus and to stand in His strength for the restoration of our corporations, cities, and our communities.

PERSONAL
COACHING

ORGANIZATIONAL
CONSULTING

LEADERSHIP
TRAINING

SPEAKING

World Class Decorum
is a collaborative
organization specializing
in Organizational
Consulting & Coaching.

World Class Decorum offers a unique approach to organizational consulting. The framework is based on the Courteous Rebel™ model of leadership developed by WCD. The foundation of our program is based on servant leadership and the desire to encourage individuals to move forward and fully prepare them to participate in the leadership relationship as both a leader and a follower. In our training we explore the nature & essence of leadership, and team members learn to apply these leadership principles & techniques to their organization.

Change Management
Mediation Training & Services
Leadership Training
Personal Coaching
Image Coaching
Professional Coaching